VORWORT

Die Vorschläge zur Leistungsmessung

Im Mittelpunkt der Unterrichtsentwicklung steht seit geraumer Zeit die Kompetenzorientierung. Die Schülerinnen und Schüler sollen nicht mehr in erster Linie gelerntes Wissen wiedergeben, sondern sie sollen zeigen, in welchem Maße sie bereits kommunikative, aber auch methodische, soziale und personale Kompetenzen beherrschen. Im Unterricht stehen die selbstständige Aneignung von Wissen und Strategien sowie die Bereitschaft und Fähigkeit zu lebenslangem Lernen im Vordergrund. Die Schüler/innen gestalten ihre Lern- und Arbeitsprozesse auf altersgemäße Weise mit und arbeiten mit anderen zusammen. Vor diesem Hintergrund spielen die Leistungsmessung und Leistungsbeurteilung eine besondere Rolle, weil sie den Lernenden eine Rückmeldung über den erreichten Lernstand geben. Während der Unterricht darauf abzielt, Kompetenzen zu erwerben, zu vertiefen und immer weiter auszudifferenzieren, soll die Lernerfolgsmessung Gelegenheit bieten, das Gelernte unter Beweis zu stellen. Klassenarbeiten sollten nach Möglichkeit eine Zusammenstellung mehrerer Teilaufgaben sein, die rezeptive und produktive Leistungen überprüfen.

Die einzelnen Aufgaben der **Vorschläge zur Leistungsmessung** sind so gestaltet, dass sie einerseits auf die sprachlichen und thematischen Bereiche der jeweiligen Unit eingehen, aber darüber hinaus auch die persönlichen Vorstellungen und Erfahrungen der Lernenden abrufen. Sie sind alters- und situationsgerecht gestaltet. Zur Bewältigung der Aufgaben erhalten die Schülerinnen und Schüler eindeutige Arbeitsanweisungen, so dass sie von Anfang an genau wissen, worauf es bei der Lösung der jeweiligen Aufgaben ankommt. Die Abfolge der Aufgaben für die einzelnen Units orientiert sich in der Regel an den Kategorien der Bildungsstandards und Lehrpläne:

Kommunikative Kompetenzen

- Hörverstehen
- Sprechen
- Leseverstehen
- Schreiben
- Sprachmittlung

Verfügbarkeit sprachlicher Mittel

- Wortschatz
- Grammatik

Die Aufgaben und Übungen, die zu jeder Unit zur Verfügung stehen, stellen ein Angebot dar, aus dem von Fall zu Fall ausgewählt werden kann oder auch ausgewählt werden muss, wenn beispielsweise bestimmte Aufgabenformate nicht in Klassenarbeiten verwendet werden sollen. Den Schwerpunkt bei der Zusammenstellung von Klassenarbeiten sollten kompetenzorientierte Aufgaben bilden.
Es gibt zu jeder Unit zwei Aufgaben zum Hörverstehen. Es können längere Hörtexte, in denen ein bestimmtes Thema zusammenhängend dargeboten wird, ebenso ausgewählt werden wie solche, die aus mehreren kurzen Hörpassagen bestehen, z. B. Telefonauskünften, Mitteilungen oder Kurzinformationen. Für Unit 2 und 3 wurden frei gesprochene Texte ohne ausformulierte Textvorlagen aufgenommen.
Zur Überprüfung des Leseverstehens werden pro Unit zwei bis vier unterschiedliche Texte angeboten. Mit Blick auf die Abschlussprüfungen am Ende der Klasse 10 sollten Klassenarbeiten auf die relevanten Prüfungsformate vorbereiten. Das ist bei allen Aufgaben und Aufgabentypen von Anfang an bedacht worden.

Um eine einzelne Kompetenz, bestimmte sprachliche Mittel oder eine bestimmte Lerntechnik zu überprüfen, kommen geschlossene Aufgabenformate zum Tragen:

- Zuordnungsaufgaben
- Selektionsaufgaben
- Transformationsaufgaben
- Lückenaufgaben

Stärker sprachproduktive Aufgaben verlangen von den Schülerinnen und Schülern

- das Beantworten von Fragen zu einem Text
- die Vervollständigung von Tabellen etc.

Offene Aufgabenformate steuern die Lösungsaktivität nur in sehr geringem Maße:

- Berichte über bestimmte Geschehnisse
- Briefe, E-Mails

Ein Grundprinzip bei der Gestaltung der kompetenzorientierten Aufgaben besteht darin, dass jeweils die Kompetenz überprüft wird, die im Mittelpunkt der jeweiligen Aufgabe steht – und möglichst nur die. Wenn es um die Überprüfung der Lesekompetenz geht, werden Aufgabentypen angeboten, die diese Fertigkeit möglichst exakt und objektiv erfassen.

Dazu gehören *multiple choice questions, matching exercises, short answer questions, true / false / not given exercises, gapped summaries*.
Wenn bei der Überprüfung der Lese- bzw. Hörverstehenskompetenz hin und wieder *write in*-Aufgaben bearbeitet werden, sollte beachtet werden, dass sprachliche Verstöße nicht zu einem Punktabzug führen, da die Kompetenz *Writing* hier nicht getestet wird. Dies erfolgt in einigen Units durch Schreibaufgaben, die im Anschluss an Hör- bzw. Lesetexte eingesetzt werden können.

Zu den Vorschlägen zur Leistungsmessung in diesem Heft gehören selbstverständlich auch Aufgaben zur Grammatik und Lexik, da die Beherrschung sprachlicher Mittel untrennbar zum Fremdsprachenerwerb gehört. Hier muss – je nach bundeslandspezifischen Anforderungen – ausgewählt werden.

In einigen Bundesländern wird in jüngster Zeit empfohlen, mindestens eine Klassenarbeit herkömmlicher Art pro Schuljahr durch eine andere gleichwertige Form zu ersetzen: Im Englischunterricht sollen in einer mündlichen Klassenarbeit die dialogische und monologische Sprechkompetenz überprüft werden. Die in diesem Heft angebotenen Aufgaben können für diese Form der alternativen Leistungsüberprüfungen verwendet werden. Den Schülerinnen und Schülern sollte dabei eine angemessene Vorbereitungszeit eingeräumt werden. Die tabellarische Übersicht auf S. 3 stellt mögliche Bewertungskriterien dar.

Im Rahmen von Klassenarbeiten spielen grundsätzlich geschlossene, halboffene und offene Aufgabenformate zusammen. Rezeptive Kompetenzen wie das Seh-/Hörverstehen und das Lesen werden im Wesentlichen in Form von geschlossenen und halboffenen Aufgaben überprüft. Im Sinne einer integrativen Überprüfung aller Kompetenzen sollten Klassenarbeiten nach Möglichkeit eine Mischung verschiedener Aufgabenformen umfassen.

Beurteilungskriterien

Es ist von besonderer Bedeutung, Leistungsfeststellungen und vor allem Klassenarbeiten so anzulegen, dass die Notengebung für die Schüler/innen transparent ist und die jeweilige Überprüfung hinreichend Erkenntnisse über die individuelle Lernentwicklung liefert. Eine kriteriengeleitete Bewertung ist einer fehlerorientierten, die z. B. von einem Fehlerquotienten ausgeht, vorzuziehen. Häufig wird zwischen einer inhaltlichen und einer sprachlichen Aufgabenbewältigung unterschieden, wobei die Gewichtung dieser beiden Bereiche von Bundesland zu Bundesland verschieden ist. Das bedeutet, dass die Vorschläge zur Bewertung individueller Schülerleistungen in diesem Heft den länderspezifischen Bestimmungen oder Fachkonferenzbeschlüssen angepasst werden müssen.

Bei der Bewertung offener Aufgaben, besonders im Bereich des Schreibens, sollten von vornherein klare und für die Schüler/innen nachvollziehbare Kriterien festgelegt werden. Sie können sich beziehen auf:

- inhaltliche Aspekte
- Genauigkeit der Kenntnisse
- Verständlichkeit der Aussagen
- sprachliche Klarheit
- gedankliche Stringenz und inhaltliche Strukturiertheit
- Reichhaltigkeit und Differenziertheit des thematischen und funktionalen Wortschatzes
- Komplexität und Variation des Satzbaus
- grammatische Korrektheit
- orthografische, lexikalische Fehler
- Verstöße gegen Sprachrichtigkeit unter Berücksichtigung einer möglichen Beeinträchtigung der Kommunikation

Die tabellarische Übersicht auf S. 4 stellt mögliche Kriterien dar, mit denen offene Aufgaben zur Überprüfung der Schreibkompetenz nachvollziehbar bewertet werden können. Die Bewertungseinheiten sind selbstverständlich Vorschläge, die individuell angepasst werden müssen, ebenso die Umsetzung in Noten. Diese muss den jeweiligen Bedingungen und rechtlichen Bestimmungen für Klassenarbeiten und Lernkontrollen entsprechen.

Zur leichteren Orientierung bei der Zusammenstellung einer Klassenarbeit oder Lernkontrolle sind in einer einleitenden tabellarischen Übersicht vor jeder Unit angegeben:

- die Seitenzahlen,
- die Titel der Aufgaben,
- Kurzbeschreibungen der Aufgaben,
- die Parts, nach deren Behandlung die Aufgabe gestellt werden kann
- die jeweils vorherrschende Kompetenz sowie
- Vorschläge zur Bepunktung der Aufgaben.

Bewertungskriterien zur Überprüfung der Grundfertigkeit „Sprechen" in Klasse 9

Punkte	Kommunikative Leistung			Inhaltliche Leistung	Sprachliche Leistung		
	Monologisches Sprechen	Dialogisches Sprechen	Redefluss	Inhalt	Sprachliche Vielfalt (Lexik und Grammatik)	Sprachliche Richtigkeit (Lexik und Grammatik)	Aussprache und Intonation
6	Kommunikative Absicht ist erfüllt; Einzelne Elemente sind verknüpft, ein linearer Aufbau ist erkennbar; Reagiert spontan auf Rückfragen; Zeigt sich – im Rahmen seiner sprachlichen Möglichkeiten – teilweise flexibel	Kann ein Gespräch beginnen, in Gang halten und beenden; Reagiert – teilweise spontan – auf den Gesprächspartner; Zeigt sich – im Rahmen seiner sprachlichen Möglichkeiten – in der Interaktion flexibel	Ist bemüht, flüssig zu sprechen; Wendet vereinzelt Gesprächsstrategien wie Rückfragen und Umschreibungen an	Inhaltliche Anforderungen sind voll erfüllt	Verfügt über die in der Aufgabe geforderte Bandbreite an Lexik und Grammatik, die sprachlichen Mittel sind jedoch begrenzt; Verknüpfungen auch mit „because"	Verstöße gegen sprachliche Korrektheit treten auf, vereinzelt auch systematische Fehler, Verständlichkeit ist aber nicht beeinträchtigt; Weitestgehende Vermeidung von Germanismen	Verständliche Aussprache; Aussprache und Intonation führen nicht zu Missverständnissen
4	Kommunikative Absicht kann erschlossen werden; Isolierte Elemente sind teilweise zwar verknüpft, der Aufbau ist jedoch nicht immer schlüssig; Kann teilweise spontan auf Rückfragen reagieren	Kann ein Gespräch beginnen und beenden; Kann Fragen stellen und auf Fragen reagieren; Rollenidentifikation vorhanden	Redefluss ist stockend; Braucht längere Bedenkzeit	Inhaltliche Anforderungen sind größtenteils erfüllt	Verfügt über elementare sprachliche Muster: Wortgruppen und sehr kurze Sätze; Verknüpfungen wie z. B. „and", „or", „but", „then"	Verstöße gegen sprachliche Normen und systematische Fehler treten auf; Gelegentliche Germanismen; Die Verständlichkeit ist teilweise beeinträchtigt	Größtenteils verständliche Aussprache; Aussprache und Intonation führen vereinzelt zu Missverständnissen
2	Kommunikative Absicht ist unter Anstrengung erschließbar; Isolierte Wendungen werden zwar teilweise verknüpft, dies erzeugt jedoch nur sehr beschränkte Linearität; Reagiert nur verzögert auf Rückfragen	Übernimmt im Gespräch eine passive Rolle; Ist davon abhängig, dass der Gesprächspartner sehr langsam spricht; Benötigt Hilfen wie Wiederholungen und Umschreibungen	Spricht wenig und sehr stockend; Braucht viel Bedenkzeit	Inhaltliche Anforderungen sind nur teilweise erfüllt	Lexik deutlich eingeschränkt und häufige Wiederholungen; Verfügt nur über sehr elementare sprachliche Muster und memorierte Wendungen; Verknüpfungen sind vorhanden, überwiegend mit demselben Konnektor	Verstöße gegen sprachliche Korrektheit und systematische Fehler treten gehäuft auf; Germanismen treten auf; Verständlichkeit ist beeinträchtigt	Aussprache teilweise unverständlich; Aussprache und Intonation führen zu Missverständnissen
0	Kommunikative Absicht ist nicht erkennbar; Keine Reaktion auf Rückfragen	Kann nicht am Gespräch teilnehmen; Reagiert nicht auf den Gesprächspartner	Spricht nicht	Inhaltliche Anforderungen sind nicht erkennbar	Lexik nicht vorhanden; Verfügt über keine sprachlichen Muster	Keine Verständigung möglich	Unverständliche Aussprache

Bewertungskriterien zur Überprüfung der Grundfertigkeit „Schreiben" in Klasse 9

	5 Punkte	4 Punkte	3 Punkte	2 Punkte	1 Punkt	0 Punkte
Textaufbau (Textsortenspezifisch/Adressatenorientiert)	Der Gedankengang ist klar, der Text ist gegliedert und liest sich flüssig, textsortenspezifische Merkmale wurden beachtet	Der Gedankengang ist klar und meist schlüssig	Der Gedankengang ist insgesamt klar, einzelne Textstellen lesen sich nicht flüssig	Der Gedankengang ist insgesamt noch klar, obwohl sich einige Textstellen nicht flüssig lesen lassen	Der Gedankengang ist an mehreren Stellen nicht klar, mehrere Textstellen lesen sich nicht flüssig	Der Gedankengang ist kaum nachvollziehbar. Der überwiegende Teil des Textes liest sich nicht flüssig
Inhalt	Aufgabenstellung beachtet; Inhaltlich richtig, vollständig und aussagekräftig, originell und kreativ	Aufgabenstellung beachtet; Inhaltlich im Wesentlichen richtig, im Wesentlichen vollständig und aussagekräftig	Aufgabenstellung im Wesentlichen beachtet; Inhaltlich überwiegend richtig	Aufgabenstellung teilweise beachtet; Inhaltlich teilweise lückenhaft, wenig aussagekräftig	Aufgabenstellung nur in Ansätzen beachtet; Inhaltlich lückenhaft, wenig aussagekräftig	Aufgabenstellung kaum beachtet; Inhaltlich bruchstückhaft/falsch, nicht aussagekräftig
Verfügbarkeit sprachlicher Mittel	Lernstufenangemessener Wortschatz und Strukturen, die situationsbezogen und differenziert verwendet werden, um das Thema/die Aufgabe zu bearbeiten; Risikobereitschaft, komplexere Strukturen zu benutzen	Wortschatz und Strukturen reichen aus, um das Thema/die Aufgabe zu bearbeiten	Wortschatz und Strukturen reichen weitgehend aus, um das Thema/die Aufgabe zu bearbeiten	Wortschatz und Strukturen reichen an einigen Stellen nicht aus, um die Aufgabe zu bearbeiten	Wortschatz und Strukturen sind sehr begrenzt und reichen an mehreren Stellen nicht aus, um das Thema zu bearbeiten	Wortschatz und Strukturen sind so begrenzt, dass sie nicht ausreichen, um das Thema/die Aufgabe zu bearbeiten
Korrektheit	Im Verhältnis zur Textlänge vereinzelte orthografische und/oder grammatische Fehler, die die Verständlichkeit nicht beeinträchtigen	Mehrere geringfügige orthografische und/oder grammatische Fehler, die die Verständlichkeit nicht wesentlich beeinflussen	Eine Vielzahl an geringfügigen und vereinzelt grobe orthografische und/oder grammatische Fehler, die die Verständlichkeit teilweise beeinflussen; Einfache Strukturen werden überwiegend korrekt verwendet, die Verständlichkeit wird nicht beeinträchtigt; Komplexere Strukturen können gelegentlich Fehler aufweisen, die Verständlichkeit kann beeinträchtigt sein	Gehäufte grobe grammatische/orthografische Fehler, die die Verständlichkeit stark beeinflussen	Gehäufte gravierende Fehler, die die Verständlichkeit stark einschränken; Einige einfache Strukturen werden korrekt verwendet, es treten viele elementare Fehler auf, es ist teilweise unklar, was ausgedrückt werden soll	Der Text ist so fehlerhaft, dass er kaum verstanden werden kann

Australia

Unit 1

Übersicht der Aufgaben

Seite	Aufgabe	Kurzbeschreibung	Kompetenz	Punkte
7/8	1 Are Australian teenagers different?	Informationen erfassen und a) Fakten zu Charlene und Oscar in eine Tabelle mit Oberbegriffen eintragen b) eine Multiple-Choice-Aufgabe zum Globalverstehen lösen c) eine E-Mail über das eigene Leben als Teenager schreiben	Hörverstehen I[1] (Nach Part C) Schreiben	18 1 20
8/9	2 Marine life	Detailinformationen erfassen und a) Notizen zu Leitfragen anfertigen b) Notizen vervollständigen c) eine Multiple-Choice-Aufgabe lösen	Hörverstehen II (Nach Part C)	8 9 3
10	3 Why not go to Australia?	Mithilfe von Bildern und Impulsen über einen Aufenthalt in Australien sprechen	Monologisches Sprechen I (Nach Part C)	20
10	4 International students in Australia	Mithilfe eines Diagramms über Studierende in Australien und deren Herkunft sprechen und die eigene Meinung zu Arbeit oder Studium in Australien äußern	Monologisches Sprechen II (Nach Part B)	20
11	5 Nice to meet you	Mithilfe von Rollenkarten ein freundliches Gespräch führen	Dialogisches Sprechen (Nach Part B)	20
12/13	6 The "stolen generations"	Die Geschichte einer Aborigine lesen und a) vier Satzanfänge vervollständigen, in denen die wichtigsten Stationen ihres Lebens nacherzählt werden b) schreiben, wie sich Janet gefühlt hat und warum c) einen möglichen Ausgang der Geschichte schreiben	Leseverstehen I (Nach Part D) Schreiben	8 9 10
14/15	7 Sydney Explorer	Einen Flyer zum *Sydney Explorer* lesen und Aussagen zu Detailinformationen als *True/False/Not given* ankreuzen	Leseverstehen II (Nach Part A)	8

---

[1] Die Transkripte der Hörtexte zu dieser Unit finden Sie als kostenloses Online-Angebot auf unserer Website **www.englishg.de** unter >Downloads<.

1

Seite	Aufgabe	Kurzbeschreibung	Kompetenz	Punkte
16/17	8 **Sydney Harbour Highlights Cruise**	Einem Flyer zu *Sydney Harbour Highlights Cruise* Detailinformationen entnehmen und Notizen zu Leitfragen anfertigen	Leseverstehen III (Nach Part A)	9
18/19	9 **The Bridge Climb**	In einem Werbetext zum *Bridge Climb* Detailaussagen erfassen und Notizen in eine Tabelle eintragen	Leseverstehen IV (Nach Part A)	14
19	10 **Extreme sports**	Mithilfe von Bildern und Impulsen sich zu Extremsportarten äußern und über die Rolle des Sports im eigenen Leben schreiben	Schreiben I (auch in Verbindung mit Aufg. 9)	20
20	11 **An e-mail from the outback**	Eine Antwortmail über den deutschen Schulalltag und wesentliche Unterschiede zur *School of the Air* schreiben	Schreiben II (Nach Part B)	20
20	12 **Learning through travel**	Einen Text schreiben und am Beispiel Australiens darstellen, wie Reisen das Leben bereichert	Schreiben III (Nach Part C)	20
21	13 **At the lost property office**	In einem Fundbüro einem deutschen Touristen helfen und in einer zweisprachigen Situation mündlich vermitteln	Sprachmittlung I (Nach Part B)	12
22	14 **Signs**	a) Die Aussage australischer Hinweisschilder auf Deutsch wiedergeben b) Die Aussage deutscher Schilder auf Englisch wiedergeben	Sprachmittlung II (Nach Part B)	8 8
23	15 **Australia – the continent "Down Under"**	Wörter zum Thema *Australia* in einen Lückentext einsetzen	Wortschatz I (Nach Part A)	7 (je 0,5)
24	16 **Preparing for a trip in Australia**	Das Wort finden, das in den Satz passt (*Multiple Choice*)	Wortschatz II (Nach Part C)	3 (je 0,5)
25	17 **What did Rob do last week?**	a) Durch einen Kalender und Bilder gesteuert über Robs Aktivitäten jede Woche und die der letzten Woche schreiben (*simple present und simple past*) b) Über eigene Aktivitäten am Wochenende schreiben (*simple present/ simple past*)	Grammatik I (Nach Part B)	14 12
26	18 **A phone call to Hong Kong**	Jeannies Aussagen zu ihrem Leben im Outback einer Freundin in indirekter Rede wiedergeben	Grammatik II (Nach Part C)	10

1 LISTENING Are Australian teenagers different?

a) Listen to Charlene and Oscar who are taking part in a phone-in radio show. Complete their fact files in 1–5 words or numbers.

_____ / 18

Name	Charlene	Oscar
Age		
Place of living	Donnybrook/Western Australia	
Parents' jobs: Dad Mum	(fruit) farmer (fruit) farmer	
Hobbies	Name three:	Name one:
Plans for the future	Name two:	Name one:
Sends greetings to (2 each)		
Music request		

b) Do Charlene and Oscar think that Australian teenagers are different from teenagers in other countries?
Tick the correct answer. There's only one correct solution.   ____/ 1

Charlene and Oscar	a) are not sure whether Australian teenagers are different from other teenagers around the world.	
	b) think that all teenagers like the same music but have different attitudes towards school.	
	c) think that teenagers are almost the same everywhere around the world.	

c) You've just listened to two Australian teenagers, Charlene and Oscar. How is your life different from theirs?   ____/ 20

Write an e-mail of about 150 words to the radio station in which you tell them about yourself.
Write about your family, hobbies and interests and about your plans for the future.
Compare your life with Charlene's and Oscar's.
Start and finish your e-mail in a friendly way.

Dear Radio Australia

2 LISTENING   Marine life 🎧2, 🎧3, 🎧4

a) Text 1: The Monkey Mia dolphins 🎧2   ____/ 8

Listen to Sarah, the guide at Monkey Mia. Answer the questions in 1–7 words or numbers. You will hear the recording twice.

1 What was this place 40 years ago? _____

2 What did the dolphins like about the place? _____

3 When did it become a national park? _____

4 How many dolphins can you usually see there in the mornings? _____

5 Which dolphins get food? _____

6 Where can you get more information about the dolphins? _____

7 What can some of the tourists do? _____

8 What are the tourists not allowed to do? _____

b) Text 2: Whale watching 🎧 3 ____/ 9

A tourist is phoning Hillary's Marina to get some information on whale watching trips.

Complete the tourist's notes with the correct words or numbers. You will hear the recording twice.

Whale watching trips

Tours take place from _____ to _____

Tours start   at _____

on _____, _____, _____ and _____

A family ticket costs _____

Chances to see whales are _____

c) Text 3: Sharks! 🎧 4 ____/ 3

Listen to Jack and his mum at the beach. Tick the correct answer. There's only one correct solution.

1 Jack's mum likes this place because	a) there are only a few people.	
	b) the sea is very quiet there.	
	c) you can see for miles.	
2 Jack's mum is worried because	a) the sun is very strong that day.	
	b) she has seen a shark in the sea.	
	c) someone has seen a shark in the sea.	
3 Jack can go swimming further up the beach because	a) there are only a few people.	
	b) there are more people.	
	c) there are lifeguards watching the sea.	

3 SPEAKING Why not go to Australia? ____/ 20

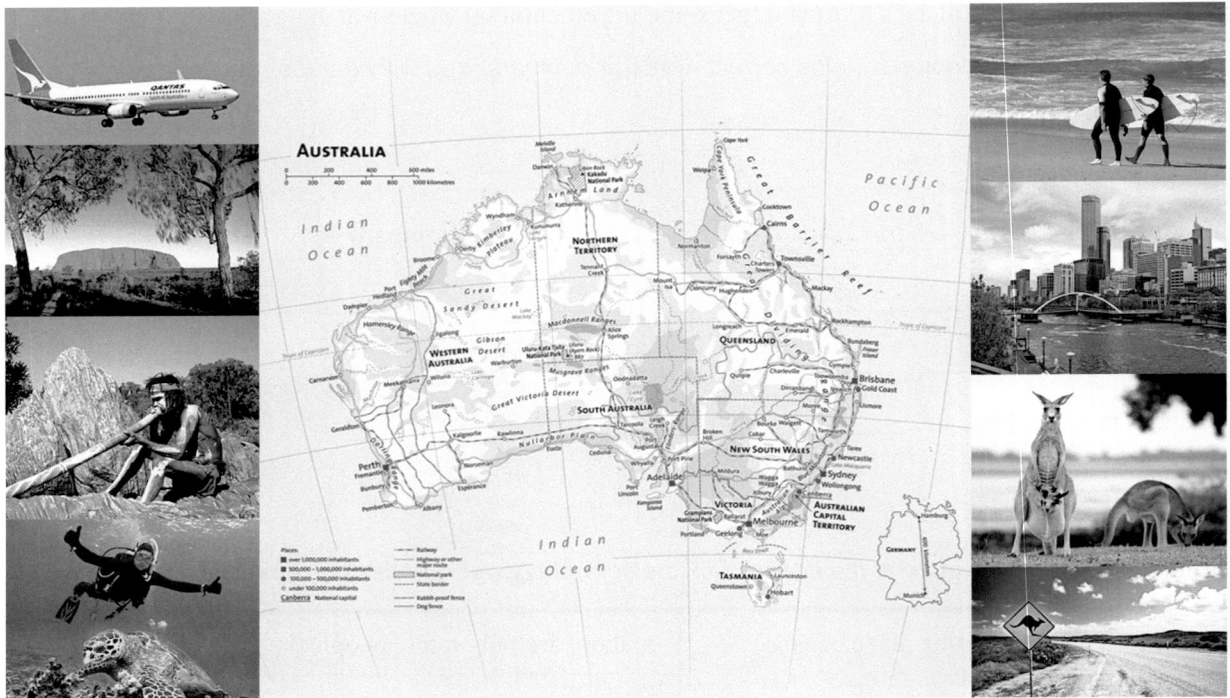

Prepare a report of about three minutes to answer the question above. Talk about interesting places in Australia and things you can do there. You've got ten minutes to prepare your talk.

Think about
- sights or attractions you should see or visit
- activities you can do there
- animals, plants or natural sights you can only see there
- the Aborigines and their traditions

Say whether you would like to go to Australia one day. Why or why not?

4 SPEAKING International students in Australia ____/ 20

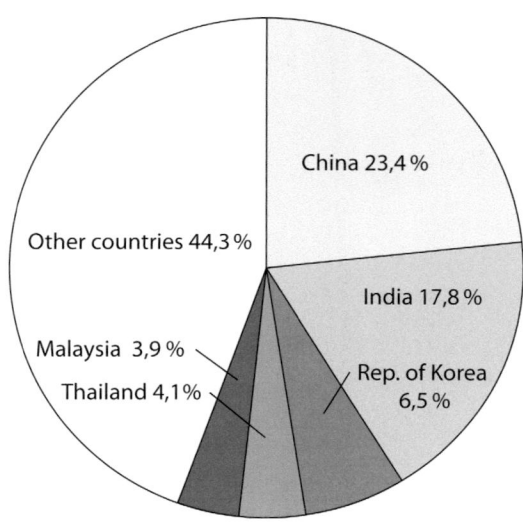

International students studying in Australia in 2008

- China 23,4 %
- India 17,8 %
- Rep. of Korea 6,5 %
- Thailand 4,1 %
- Malaysia 3,9 %
- Other countries 44,3 %

*Say what the pie chart shows.
Give details and finish with a conclusion. Speculate where the "Other students" might come from.*

What does working or studying in Australia mean for young people?

Say whether you would like to work or study there one day. Why (not)?

Talk for about three minutes. You've got ten minutes to prepare your talk.

Source: www.studiesinaustralia.com (April 2010)

1

5 SPEAKING   Nice to meet you   ____ / 20

Prepare and act out the role play below with your partner.

Imagine you've just met for the first time.
Start your conversation very politely.
Introduce yourselves to each other.
Make small talk.
Ask or give help.
End your conversation in a friendly way. You've got ten minutes to prepare your dialogue.

Partner A   ✂ **Partner B**

You're in town walking across the market place.
You see another tourist who has rented a bike.
You want to know where she/he rented it and ask how to get there.
You're also interested in a cycle tour and you're planning to buy some maps for such tours.

You're a tourist.
You're sitting on a bench with a bike next to you.
You've just rented the bike.
You're looking at some maps for cycle tours.
The next day you want to start a cycle tour for a few days.
It would be nice to go with someone.

OR

Prepare and act out the role play below with your partner.

Imagine you've just met for the first time.
Start your conversation very politely.
Introduce yourselves to each other.
Make small talk.
Ask or give help.
End your conversation in a friendly way. You've got ten minutes to prepare your dialogue.

Partner A   ✂ **Partner B**

You're on a cycle tour on your way to …
You meet a cyclist who is taking a rest.
He/She is looking at a map.
You offer your help.
You know a nice hostel only half an hour away.
You want to stay there too.
You offer to go there together.

You're on a cycle tour.
It's late in the afternoon.
You're taking a rest and are looking at your map.
You're looking for a place to stay.
You ask partner A about cheap accommodation.

6 READING The "stolen generations"

Janet is part of Australian's "stolen generations". These were Aborigines and mixed-race children who were taken from their families between 1869 and 1970.

Read the text about her experiences growing up.

Janet couldn't remember what her mother and father looked like. She was too young, just five years old, the last time she saw them. For years she was told she was an orphan, but one day she received a letter from an aunt. The day she received the letter, Janet's world collapsed. Her parents hadn't died when she was a child. They had spent years looking for her, her aunt wrote. One day, fifteen years ago, Janet's
5 father had taken his daughter to hospital. She was ill and her parents were worried. The doctors told Janet's father that she had to stay in hospital and they sent him home. That was the last time they saw each other.

Janet was taken to a special home run by the church where there were lots of other Aboriginal children. The people who ran the home were cruel. They punished Janet because she called for her mother at
10 night. She wasn't allowed to eat. Sometimes they beat her. They told the children that the dark-skinned Aborigines were not as good as the white Australians.

When she was seven, Janet went to live with a family in Darwin. Her new "parents" were kind and said that they loved her, but she always felt that she was different to them. At school the other children didn't talk to her. Some of them called her names because of her dark skin. If Janet asked about her real
15 family, they always told her the same. Her parents were dead and the rest of the family was too poor to look after her. They told her she was lucky. She had a new family now and a new future.

That new future disappeared the day she found out who she really was. Her parents had never given up hope. They knew she was alive somewhere. Janet's father went back to the hospital many times, but the doctors said they didn't know where Janet was. Over the years they searched for Janet everywhere they
20 could. It was difficult to find help. Finally, after many years, Janet's aunt found out where she was living and wrote her a letter. Her parents were both very ill, but they hoped to see her. The aunt sent her an address and a telephone number. Janet didn't know what to think. She didn't know what to do. But she did know that her life would never be the same again.

a) *Read the text and complete the sentences about the most important steps in Janet's life.* ____ / 8

1 When Janet was five years old, _____

_____

_____

2 Until she was seven _____

_____

_____

3 Then _____

_____

_____

4 When she was 20, _____

_____

_____

b) *Write how Janet felt and why she felt like that. Use your own words. Do not copy the text.* ____ / 9

How did Janet feel …

1 … when she lived in the children's home? _____

Why? _____

_____

2 … when she lived with her new family in Darwin? _____

Why? _____

_____

3 …when she received her aunt's letter? _____

Why? _____

_____

c) *What do you think Janet did after she got her aunt's letter? (Did she leave the family in Darwin? Did she meet her parents?)* ____ / 10
Write an ending to the story in about 60 words.

7 READING Sydney Explorer ____/ 8

Sydney Explorer Hop-on Hop-off sightseeing bus

The 'red' Sydney Explorer bus visits **27 of Sydney's most famous attractions** such as the Opera House, Royal Botanic Gardens, Mrs Macquarie's Chair, Kings Cross, The Rocks, Darling Harbour and a lot more.

It is the only timetabled hop-on hop-off sightseeing bus that stops north of the harbour and travels across the Sydney Harbour Bridge.

Each Sydney Explorer is air-conditioned and includes on-board commentary, giving you fascinating insights into the history and culture of Sydney.

This service can be picked up at any stop along the route. You can hop on or off as you please, then simply catch the next bus when it arrives. Each bus operates[1] at 20-minute intervals. Allow two hours to complete the entire journey.

Tickets include unlimited travel on both the Sydney Explorer and the **Bondi Explorer** as well as regular Sydney Buses services in the **Blue TravelPass zone**. Tickets are valid until 4 am on the following day.

Your Explorer ticket also entitles[2] you to fantastic **discount offers** at a variety of attractions and venues on route.

Costs			
Service	Adult	Child*	Family**
Combined Sydney Explorer/Bondi Explorer			
1 day ticket	Retail[3] $ 39.00	Retail $ 19.00	Retail $ 97.00
2 day ticket	Retail $ 70.00	Retail $ 35.00	Retail $ 175.00
* Child 4–15 years of age. Under 4 years travels free.			
** Family 2 adults and any number of children from the same family.			

http://www.sydneybuses.info/tourist-services/sydney-explorer.htm

---

[1] (to) operate *verkehren*
[2] (to) entitle sb. to sth. *jdn. zu etw. berechtigen*
[3] retail *Ladenpreis*

Read the Sydney Explorer website. Then decide if the statements are true, false or not given. Tick the correct box.

	True	False	Not given
1 The Sydney Explorer also takes you across the Sydney Harbour Bridge.			
2 On the bus, you'll learn a lot about Sydney.			
3 You can listen to a commentary in different languages.			
4 There are buses every half hour.			
5 There are buses every day of the year.			
6 The last Sydney Explorer bus is at midnight.			
7 You'll pay less for many attractions with your Explorer ticket.			
8 A family ticket includes not more than three children.			

8 READING Sydney Harbour Highlights Cruise   ___/ 9

Sydney Harbour Highlights Cruise

- ★★★⯪☆ based on 21 reviews
- Duration: 90 minutes (approx.)
- Location: Sydney, Australia
- Product code: 3378HIGH

See Sydney's highlights on a 1.5-hour cruise along Sydney Harbour. What better introduction to the Harbour City do you need? With a choice of four departure times, you can plan your day to suit yourself. You'll see Sydney's must-see attractions from the water on a comprehensive introductory tour, giving you a great overview of Sydney and leaving you time in the day to explore on your own.

Relax in style as you see all the points of interest on Sydney Harbour's Main Harbour. You'll cruise past the Sydney Opera House to Double Bay, exclusive Point Piper, Bradley Head, under the Sydney Harbour Bridge to Balmain and Darling Harbour. Along the way you'll receive detailed commentary about the sights on the harbour.

The family-friendly Sydney Harbour Highlights Cruise is perfect for all travellers and a fabulous introduction to Sydney and its harbour.

Schedule details

Departure point:
Circular Quay, located in downtown Sydney

Return details:
Returns to original departure point

Departure time:
11.00 am   2.30 pm
12.45 pm   4.30 pm

www.partner.viator.com/en/1422/tours/Sydney/Sydny-Harbour-Highlights-Guide/d357-3378HIGH

Read the website text. Find the missing information. Then answer the questions in 1–3 words or numbers:

The Sydney Harbour Highlights Cruise	
1 How long does the cruise take?	
2 How many times a day do the boats run?	
3 What can you see? (Name three things.)	1 _____ 2 _____ 3 _____
4 Who is the offer for? (Name two.)	1 _____ 2 _____
5 Where do the boats start from?	
6 Where does the cruise end?	

9 READING The Bridge Climb   ____ / 14

If you like to combine sightseeing and sports on your travels, the Sydney Bridge Climb might be the right challenge.

Sydney Harbour Bridge is probably one of the best-
5 known Australian landmarks. It was opened in 1932.

Until 1998 only workers maintaining Sydney Harbour Bridge were allowed to climb the steel arch of the bridge, but in October 1998 it was opened to the public. The "Bridge Climb" is now one of the most popular Sydney
10 attractions. Over two million people have climbed the bridge since it was opened, although it is quite an expensive adventure.

You can only climb it in a group. Guided tours are offered every day except 30 and 31 December. They are run in almost all weather conditions. Only thunderstorms and very strong winds make climbs
15 impossible.

The climb takes tourists along the upper part of the arch all the way to the top, 134 metres above Sydney Harbour and offers fantastic views of the harbour and the city. On a bright day you can see the Pacific Ocean in the east and the Blue Mountains in the west.

Climbers can choose from four different climbing times: "Dawn" (offered on the first Saturday of the
20 month), "Day", "Twilight" and "Night" – all these are offered every day except 30 and 31 December. "Bridge Climb" tickets are for a specific date and time and must be booked in advance. Bookings can be made online or on the telephone.

The climb takes three and a half hours from checking-in to returning to the starting point.

Climbers must arrive 15 minutes before their climb time to check in.

25 Climbers must be over 10 years of age, and children up to the age of 15 must be accompanied by an adult at all times. Anybody taking part in the climb must be taller than 1.20 m.

Climbers have to wear a special "Bridge Suit" over their own clothing. Lockers are provided, as small, loose objects such as
30 cameras or video recorders cannot be taken onto the bridge.

Climbers must wear rubber-soled shoes such as running, sports or hiking shoes.

All climbers receive a group photograph.

Read the text and complete the table.

The Bridge Climb	
1 First public bridge climb	
2 Reasons for stopping the climbs. (Name two.)	1 _____ 2 _____
3 Reasons for doing the climb (Name two.)	1 _____ 2 _____
4 Offered dates	
5 Ways of booking (Name two.)	1 _____ 2 _____
6 Duration of the climb	
7 Climbers must be …	1 _____ 2 _____ 3 _____
8 Rules for clothes (Name two.)	1 _____ 2 _____

10 WRITING   Extreme sports _____/ 20

Here are three unusual sports. Write what you think about them and why. Write about:

- *what they have in common*
- *why people do these kinds of sport*
- *which of them is the most dangerous and why*

Then write about the role of sport in your life. Would you like to try an extreme sport? If so, which one? If not, why not? Write 150–180 words.

11 WRITING An e-mail from the outback   ____ / 20

Imagine you got this e-mail from Jeannie in Australia.

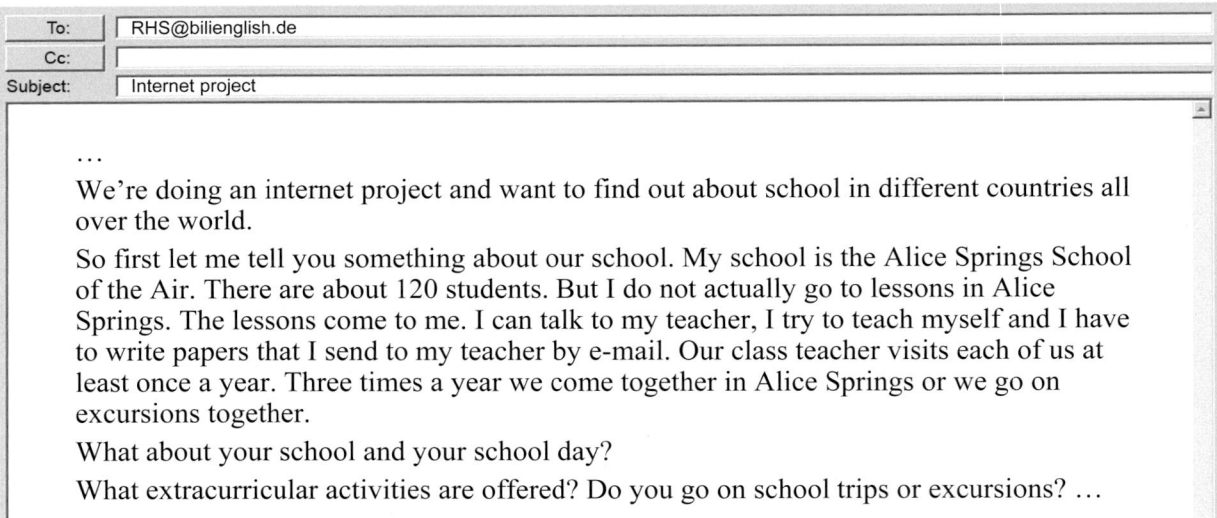

> …
>
> We're doing an internet project and want to find out about school in different countries all over the world.
>
> So first let me tell you something about our school. My school is the Alice Springs School of the Air. There are about 120 students. But I do not actually go to lessons in Alice Springs. The lessons come to me. I can talk to my teacher, I try to teach myself and I have to write papers that I send to my teacher by e-mail. Our class teacher visits each of us at least once a year. Three times a year we come together in Alice Springs or we go on excursions together.
>
> What about your school and your school day?
>
> What extracurricular activities are offered? Do you go on school trips or excursions? …

Now write an e-mail of about 150 words to Jeannie in which you answer her questions.
Describe your school life and point out the differences between your school and the School of the Air.
Say what you like about your school and why.
Ask Jeannie three questions about her school.
Start and finish your e-mail in a friendly way.

12 WRITING Learning through travel   ____ / 20

Lots of people dream of a trip to Australia.

Write a text of about 150 words. Structure your text: think of a beginning, a middle and an end.
Explain why a trip "Down Under" can be a great experience and what you can learn from it.

You can write about

- places worth visiting
- things to do
- animals or natural sights to see
- other interesting facts about the continent
- …

Say whether you would or wouldn't like to go there.

13 MEDIATION   At the lost property office[1] 🎧 5   ____ / 12

A German tourist can't find his digital camera. He is at the lost property office.

Listen to the conversation and help the tourist and the clerk to understand each other.

Tourist	Danke, dass du mir hilfst. Ich kann den australischen Akzent nicht gut verstehen.
Clerk	What can I do for you?
Tourist	Ehm, ich bin zu aufgeregt. Sag du, dass ich meine Digitalkamera verloren habe.
You	My friend _____
Clerk	I see. …
You	_____
Tourist	Heute …
You	_____
Clerk	What …?
You	_____
Tourist	Es ist …
You	_____
Clerk	Sorry …
You	_____
Clerk	Have …
You	_____
Tourist	Nein …
You	_____
Clerk	Come …
You	_____
Tourist	OK. …
You	_____
Clerk	We …
You	_____
Tourist	Vielen …
You	_____
Clerk	Good luck.

---

[1] lost property office *Fundbüro*

14 MEDIATION Signs

a) Schau dir diese Schilder an und erkläre deiner Mutter auf Deutsch, worauf sie hinweisen. ____/ 8

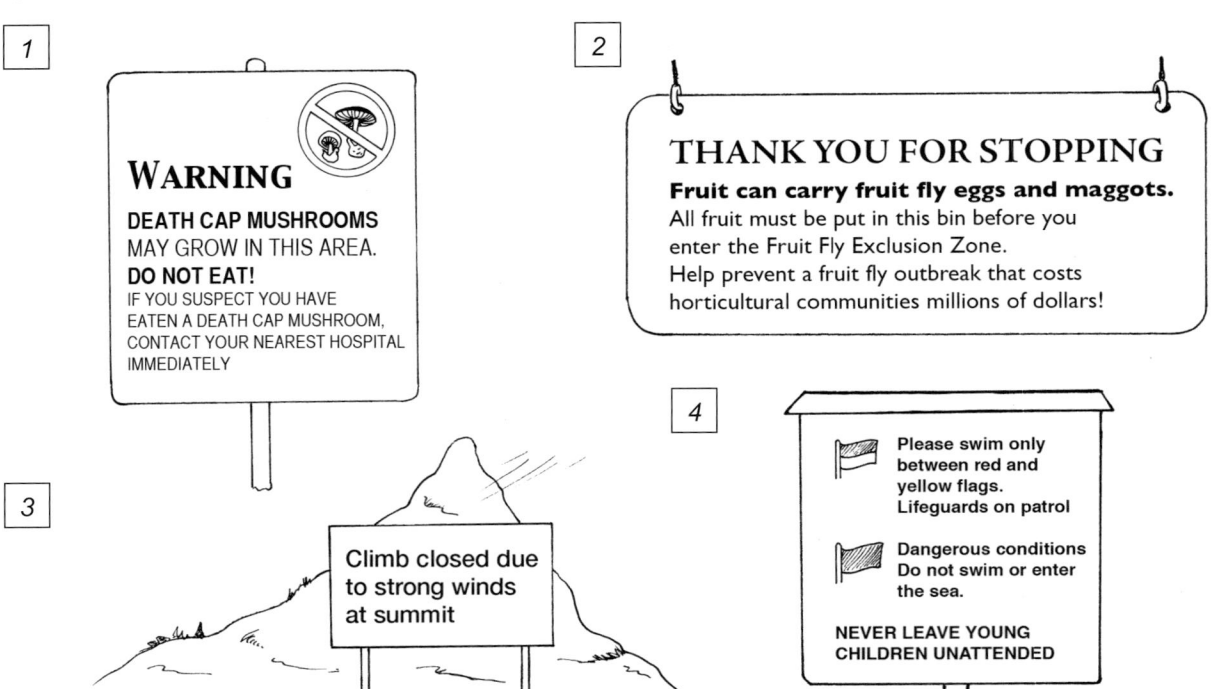

1 Auf dem ersten Schild …

b) Now help an Australian tourist with these German signs.
Tell him/her in English what they mean. ____/ 8

1 It says on this sign that …

15 WORDS Australia – the continent "Down Under"   ___/ 7

Complete the text with words from the box. There are two more words than you need. Be careful about the correct form of the nouns and verbs.

> Aborigines • area • (to) avoid • because of • cancer • desert • disease • (to) divide sth. into • flag • historical • independent • nationality • nearly • outdoors • prisoners • sunscreen

Australia is the smallest continent but one of the largest countries in the world. It has an _____ of more than 7.6 million square km. It is _____ six states and two territories. The _____ with the British Union Jack in its top left-hand corner shows Australia's _____ links with Britain.

The _____ were Australia's first settlers before the Europeans arrived. Lots of them were killed or died of _____ the Europeans brought with them. In 1788 Australia became a British colony for _____. In 1901 the country "Down Under" became _____.

Today it is a place where people of different _____ like English, German, Greek or Japanese live together. It is also an attractive place for tourists _____ its natural sights. One of the most famous attractions is the Great Barrier Reef with corals and _____ 1,500 kinds of fish. Australians and tourists love being _____ in the bush or at the beaches. But you have to be careful in the sun. More and more people are getting skin _____ because of the dangerous UV rays. So _____ the sun between 10 am and 2 pm.

16 WORDS Preparing for a trip in Australia   ____/ 3

Tick the right word to complete the sentences.

1 For my weekend in the bush I'll ask a friend about his sleeping bag. I hope I can _____ it.
   a) ☐ rent   b) ☐ borrow   c) ☐ lend   d) ☐ attach

2 Tourists are welcome to visit Uluru but they should _____ Aboriginal land.
   a) ☐ respect   b) ☐ enjoy   c) ☐ touch   d) ☐ leave

3 Before you go outdoors during the day, you should _____ sunscreen.
   a) ☐ agree on   b) ☐ put on   c) ☐ slip on   d) ☐ take on

4 I've found some figures and information about the population of the different areas in Australia for our Geography project. I'll send you an e-mail and _____ a bar chart.
   a) ☐ avoid   b) ☐ put in   c) ☐ put on   d) ☐ attach

5 For our trip through the outback we're going to _____ a caravan.
   a) ☐ pay   b) ☐ rent   c) ☐ lend   d) ☐ sell

6 I've found various offers for caravans from different companies. Which one do you _____?
   a) ☐ mean   b) ☐ advise   c) ☐ recommend   d) ☐ explain

17 GRAMMAR What did Rob do last week?

Look at Rob's weekly planner to find out what he usually does during the week.

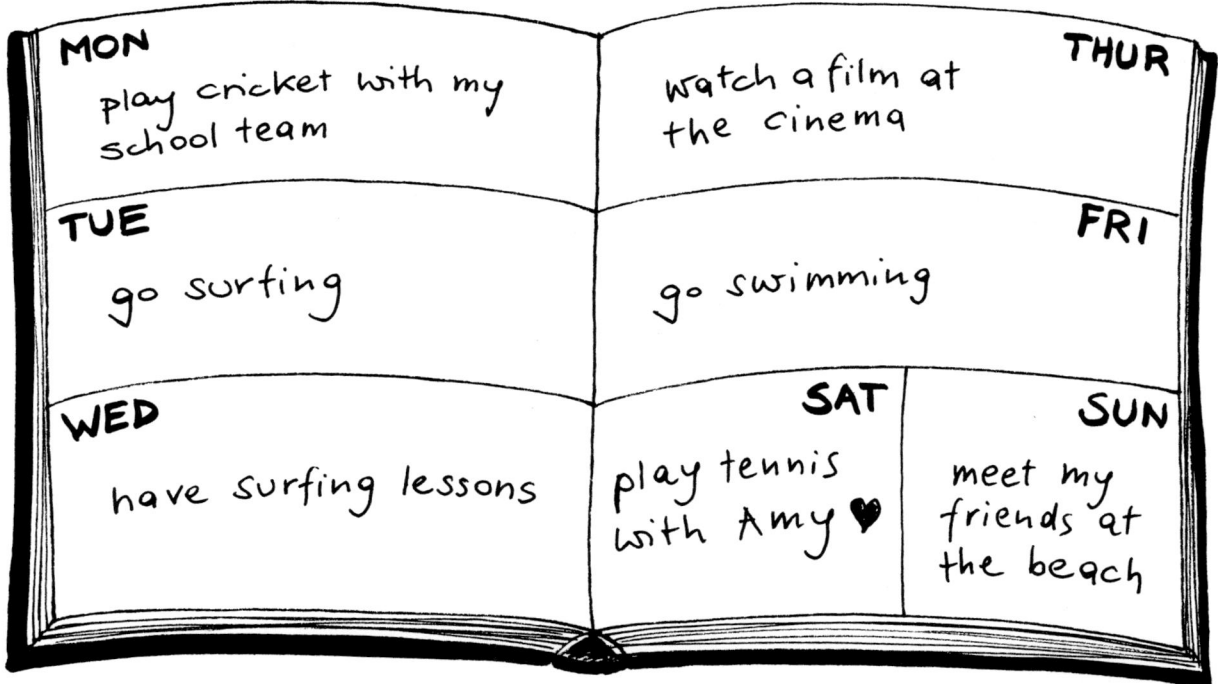

a) Last week was different for Rob. He was on a hiking trip with his class.
Look at the pictures below. Write sentences for each day. First say what he usually does using his weekly planner above. Then say what he or his classmates did. ____ / 14

On Monday Rob usually ..., but last Monday he ...

b) What about you? Write three sentences about what you usually do at the weekend. Then write three sentences about your last weekend. Say what you did and/or what you didn't do. Say why. ____ / 12

18 GRAMMAR A phone call to Hong Kong

_____ / 10

Jeannie is phoning her online friend Cath in Hong Kong. Later Cath's friend Isabel asks about Jeannie and wants to know what she told her.

Write down what Cath told Isabel.

I like my life in the outback although sometimes I'm a bit lonely.
I don't usually get up before eight.
I usually work for school in the mornings.
Last Monday I rode my motorbike to the dog fence to help my dad.
So I had to do my work for school in the evening.
In June we're going on an excursion to a camp near Darwin.
I'm really looking forward to seeing my classmates there.
I'm sure we will have lots of fun.
I hope the weather will be fine.

Use different verbs like: She went on to say … / She added … / She told me … / She hoped … / …

Jeannie said that …
She …

The world of work

Unit 2

Übersicht der Aufgaben

Seite	Aufgabe	Kurzbeschreibung	Kompetenz	Punkte
29/30	1 **Megan's work experience**	Informationen erfassen und a) Fragen zum Text beantworten b) das richtige Satzende finden c) ein Formular ausfüllen oder d) eine Multiple-Choice-Aufgabe lösen	Hörverstehen I[1] (Nach Part C)	6 5 10 5
31/32	2 **Placements for work experience**	Detailinformationen erfassen und a) Aussagen als *True/False* ankreuzen oder b) eine Multiple-Choice-Aufgabe lösen	Hörverstehen II (Nach Part C)	12 6
33	3 **An interview**	Mithilfe von Impulsen sich in einem Vorstellungsgespräch darstellen	Monologisches Sprechen (Nach Part C)	20
33	4 **A summer job**	Mithilfe von Rollenkarten ein Gespräch für einen Sommerjob führen	Dialogisches Sprechen (Nach Part C)	20
34/35	5 **A year as a volunteer in Doncaster**	Den Brief einer Gastmutter lesen und Aussagen zu Detailinformationen als *True/False/Not given* ankreuzen	Leseverstehen I (Nach Part B)	12
36	6 **Work experience – how it can help you**	Einem Text Informationen zu Praktika entnehmen und die richtigen Satzenden finden	Leseverstehen II (Nach Part C)	4
37	7 **Julia Meyer's report**	Einen Bericht über ein Praktikum lesen und eine Multiple-Choice-Aufgabe lösen	Leseverstehen III (Nach Part C)	4
38	8 **Work experience in Germany**	Zwei Berichten über Praktika Detailinformationen entnehmen und Aussagen als *True/False/Not given* ankreuzen	Leseverstehen IV (Nach Part C)	8

---

[1] Die Hörtexte zu dieser Unit wurden frei gesprochen anhand einer vorgegebenen Situation, d. h. ohne ausformulierte Textvorlage aufgenommen. Sie liegen deshalb nicht in schriftlicher Form vor.

2

Seite	Aufgabe	Kurzbeschreibung	Kompetenz	Punkte
38	9 **The right job for me**	Mithilfe von Impulsen einen Text zur Bewerbung für einen Job schreiben	Schreiben I (Nach Part A)	20
39	10 **A letter of application for a summer job**	Nach dem Lesen einer Anzeige einen Bewerbungsbrief (*formal letter*) schreiben	Schreiben II (Nach Part B)	20
39	11 **A summer job in the USA**	Einer Anzeige für einen Sommerjob in den USA Informationen entnehmen und auf Deutsch weitergeben	Sprachmittlung I (Nach Part A)	12
40	12 **A summer job at a theme park**	In einer zweisprachigen Situation zwischen Mutter und englischem Freund vermitteln	Sprachmittlung II (Nach Part C)	16
41	13 **Say it in English**	Satzinhalte auf Englisch wiedergeben	Wortschatz I (Nach Part D)	10
41	14 **What do they do?**	Tätigkeiten einzelner Berufe beschreiben	Wortschatz II (Nach Part A)	6
42	15 **Looking for a job**	Wörter zum Thema „Bewerbung" in einen Lückentext einsetzen bzw. richtig ankreuzen	Wortschatz III (Nach Part C)	9
43	16 **An interview for a summer job**	In einen Lückentext die richtige Verbform einsetzen (indirekte Rede)	Grammatik I (Nach Part C)	9
43	17 **The reality TV show**	Aufforderungen in indirekte Rede übertragen	Grammatik II (Nach Part C)	8
44	18 **At the tea shop**	a) Mrs Browns Fragen aus dem Bewerbungsgespräch in indirekter Rede wiedergeben b) Melissas Fragen an Mrs Brown in indirekter Rede wiedergeben	Grammatik III (Nach Part C)	6 6

1 LISTENING Megan's work experience 🎧6, 🎧7, 🎧8

a) Dialogue 1 🎧6   ___ / 6

Read the task. Then listen to the dialogue and answer the questions in 1–5 words or numbers. You will hear the recording twice.

1 Who is phoning the hospital? _____

2 Who does she have an interview with? _____

3 When is it? (Day/time?) _____

4 How does she get there from the tube station? (Name two facts.) _____

_____

b) Dialogue 2 🎧7   ___ / 5

Read the task. Then listen to the dialogue and match the beginnings and endings of the sentences. There are three more endings than you need.

1 Megan is	A because she is a bit early.
2 The receptionist is	B on the 5th floor on the right.
3 The office is	C speaking to Mrs Carter.
4 She can use the lift	D sending Megan up to Mrs Carter's office.
5 Megan has to wait	E speaking to Megan on the phone.
	F at the end of the hall.
	G on the 3rd floor on the right.
	H speaking to the receptionist.

| 1 | | 2 | | 3 | | 4 | | 5 | |

c) Dialogue 3 🎧8   ___ / 10

Read the task. Listen to the dialogue and fill in the form.

Queen Mary's Hospital

Applicant's name: _____

Education: _____ St. Mary's in Taddington

_____ Collingwood High School

Part-time jobs (Name two.): _____

Interests (Name two.):   _____

taking care of cats and dogs, backgammon

Working time: from _____ to _____

Work experience: _____

OR

d) Dialogue 3 🎧 8   ___/ 5

Listen to the dialogue and tick the correct ending.

1 Mrs Carter has to fill out	a) a test.	
	b) a form.	
	c) a letter.	
	d) an advertisement.	
2 Megan has done	a) some part-time jobs.	
	b) lots of part-time jobs.	
	c) work experience at a shoe shop.	
	d) work experience at a café.	
3 Megan's interests include	a) running and volleyball.	
	b) volleyball and newspapers.	
	c) volleyball and backgammon.	
	d) backgammon and running.	
4 When Megan visited her grandmother in hospital the year before,	a) she wanted to talk to her.	
	b) she decided to come and work there.	
	c) she had to help her.	
	d) she talked to the doctors and nurses.	
5 Megan's day at the hospital	a) will be very hard.	
	b) will start at 7 am.	
	c) will start at 7 am and finish at 7 pm.	
	d) will start at 8 am and finish at 7 pm.	

2 LISTENING Placements for work experience 🎧 9

a) *Read the task. Then listen to the dialogue and tick whether the statements are true or false.*

___/ 12

Jamie…	True	False
1 …is feeling great.		
2 …has already tried to find a work experience placement.		
3 …thinks it's difficult to find something that interests him.		
4 …is on the internet all day.		
5 …promises to look for a computer company.		
6 …is interested in doing game programming.		

Megan…	True	False
1 …is telling Jamie about her work experience placement.		
2 …has already had her interview.		
3 …is really excited about starting her work experience.		
4 …wants to become a doctor.		
5 …suggests contacting a computer company.		
6 …is going to talk to Jamie every day.		

OR

b) Read the task. Then listen to the dialogue and tick the correct ending. ___/ 6

1 Jamie says he is feeling	a) a little down.	
	b) all right.	
	c) great.	
	d) a bit tired.	
2 He has been looking around	a) and has contacted a computer company.	
	b) but hasn't found a work experience placement yet.	
	c) and has spoken to some people at a computer company.	
	d) but he hasn't looked at the yellow pages yet.	
3 Megan got a placement	a) at the hospital where she really wants to work.	
	b) at a hospital with lots of patients who had an accident.	
	c) at a hospital with lots of modern technology.	
	d) at a hospital for emergencies only.	
4 She can't wait to start because	a) she wants to talk to the patients.	
	b) she wants to meet other people at the hospital.	
	c) she wants to be a nurse.	
	d) she likes to see blood everywhere.	
5 She is excited about	a) starting her work experience.	
	b) the interview.	
	c) helping Jamie.	
	d) talking to the doctors.	
6 Jamie thinks it will be difficult	a) to work with computers.	
	b) to contact a computer company.	
	c) to talk to Megan.	
	d) to find something that interests him.	

3 SPEAKING An interview

_____ / 20

Imagine you are going for a job interview.

Prepare what you are going to tell the interviewer about

- your education
- your qualifications (school, subjects, work experience)
- your interests and hobbies
- why you are interested in the job
- why you think this is the right job for you
- …

Talk for about three minutes. You've got ten minutes to prepare your talk.

4 SPEAKING A summer job

_____ / 20

Partner A

You are interested in a job as a junior child-care assistant in a big hotel on Majorca.
You call Chris Brown (Partner B) who is the manager of the hotel.

Prepare and act out a dialogue of about three minutes. Remember to start and finish your call in a friendly way. You've got ten minutes to prepare your dialogue.

You want to find out
- where exactly the hotel is
- when you can work there and for how long
- what your duties would be
- about your free time
- how much money you would earn

You have to answer questions about your interests and work experience too.

Partner B

Your name is Chris Brown. You are the manager of a big hotel on Majorca. Partner A is interested in a job as a junior childcare assistant in your hotel in the summer holidays.

Prepare and act out a dialogue of about three minutes. Remember to start and finish your call in a friendly way. You've got ten minutes to prepare your dialogue.

Answer Partner A's questions about
- Location: in Palma de Majorca
- Time: from 20th July to 17th August
- Free time: one day per week
- Pay: € 300
- Duties: organizing activities like swimming, dancing, competitions; taking kids to the beach, playing games with them, …

Ask Partner A about his/her interests and work experience.

5 READING A year as a volunteer in Doncaster   ____ / 12

Katharina Flamm is going to spend a year in England. She is going to work as a volunteer in the Red Cross shop in Doncaster. She has been given the address of her host family and has written them a letter. This is the answer her host mother sends her:

Dear Katharina

Thank you so much for your friendly letter and for telling us about yourself. It's so nice for my husband and me to find out about our new 'guest daughter', we feel we already know you quite well.
Since you asked, let me tell you something about ourselves. We – that's me, Claire, my husband Christopher and our dog Rusty – are very much looking forward to meeting you. We're a little bit younger than your parents: I'm 31, Christopher is 35 and Rusty is 2 years old. (We don't have a cat, so don't worry!) I'm the shop manager of the Red Cross shop in Doncaster and Christopher is a doctor at Doncaster Royal Infirmary, our local hospital.
We haven't got any children. That's why we like to have 'guest children'. You come from a very large family – I hope you'll be OK without any 'brothers' or 'sisters' in the house. Christopher and I have friends with children your age and they're all looking forward to meeting you. The rest of our family, that's my brother Frank and his wife Judith, live near us, and they've got three young children: Emily is 2 and George and Connor are 5 – they're twins. My mother, Valerie, also lives close by and she is also looking forward to meeting her 'guest granddaughter'. I'm sure you won't feel lonely with so many people around you.

Christopher and I have a nice house in Doncaster, with a big garden – which is great for Rusty. You'll have your own room and your own bathroom too. As I said, I work at the Red Cross shop in Doncaster, so I can take you there on the first day. I don't work in the shop every day, so when I'm not working you can cycle into town. It's not far (about 15 minutes) and we have a bike which you can use. On the first day we'll teach you everything you need to know. The other volunteers are very friendly. I'm sure you'll have a great time. Doncaster is a lovely city. It's good that you're interested in history because there are lots of interesting places for you to visit. Doncaster isn't far from Leeds, which is a very big, exciting city with lots of great shops!
Thank you for the photograph of you and your family – I'm sending you a photograph of Christopher, Rusty and me, so that you and your parents can see what your host family is like.
Please say hello to your parents from us, and tell them that we'll look after you while you're staying with us.
Yours
Claire

What did Katharina tell her host family and what does she find out about them?
Tick the correct column.

	True	False	Not given
1 She has never been to England before.			
2 How old her parents are.			
3 She wants to know whether they have a dog, as she is allergic to them.			
4 What her future host parents do for a living.			
5 How many cousins she has.			
6 That she has lots of friends.			
7 Whether she will have her own room.			
8 That she loves cycling.			
9 How many hours she will work every day.			
10 How she will get to Leeds to go shopping.			
11 What the other people in the shop are like.			
12 That she was sending a photograph of her family.			

6 READING Work experience – how it can help you ___/4

Work experience can be a great help if you're still wondering what sort of career you want.

A work placement is your opportunity to spend a period of time outside the classroom, learning about a particular job or area of work.

During your placement, you'll be able to find out what skills employers look for when they're hiring someone to fill a job vacancy.

You will also get the chance to develop your self-confidence and communication skills. This will help you to work better with other people in further or higher education, as well as in your future career.

With schools, work placements are only available in Years 10 or 11. You won't be able to do a work placement with your school until you reach this age.

htttp://www.direct.gov.uk/en/EducationAndLearning/14To19/Years10And11/DG_10013569

Match the beginnings and endings correctly. There is one more ending than you need.

1 If you don't know what you want to be when you leave school,	A you can find out what employers look for when they choose people for jobs.
2 Work experience is helpful because	B you have to be of a certain age.
3 You have the chance to develop self-confidence	C you should think about looking for a work placement.
4 If you want to look for a work placement with your school,	D you will be told what is the best job for you.
	E which will help you in your future career.

1 [ ]   2 [ ]   3 [ ]   4 [ ]

7 READING Julia Meyer's report   ___/ 4

I did my work experience at the Early Years Childcare Centre in Exeter, Great Britain. I spent nine months there.

Before I applied for the position, I talked to other students who had done this in the years before, because I wasn't sure whether my English was good enough to work with young British children. The students told me that they had really enjoyed working at the Childcare Centre and that their English had become much better in a very short time. They also said that the children had loved to explain things to them which made learning English very easy. That is what I hoped for too, and indeed I am much better now.

The kindergarten in Exeter is in a converted Victorian schoolhouse with nice front and rear gardens. The back garden is walled-in and there is a play area for the children where they can play outside every day. They have places for 51 children who are looked after in three groups from babies to pre-school children.

During my work experience I had to work six hours a day from Monday to Friday. I spent about three months in each of the three groups so that I worked with babies as well as with pre-school children. I did all the jobs that were necessary in the different age groups: I changed the babies' nappies, dressed and fed them and sang songs to them. I went for walks with the older children, read books to them and played games with them. And when they asked, I helped them put on their clothes and shoes. Sometimes I also had to help them sort out an argument.

Everybody was very friendly to me and I felt accepted in the group from the very beginning. I really enjoyed my work experience. I learned a lot about the work in a British kindergarten and I practised my English.

Tick the correct box.

1 Julia talked to other students	a) to practise her English.	
	b) to find out what the job would be like.	
	c) to tell them about her plans.	
	d) to get information for her application.	
2 Julia was told that	a) she was too old for the job.	
	b) her English was not good enough.	
	c) learning English from young children was fun.	
	d) she could only stay at the Centre for a short time.	
3 Julia did lots of jobs, e.g.	a) reading to the children.	
	b) cleaning the play area.	
	c) washing the children's clothes.	
	d) teaching the children to read.	
4 In the end Julia knew	a) a lot about the work in an English kindergarten.	
	b) that it is not easy to work with children.	
	c) that working in a kindergarten is not much fun.	
	d) a lot of English songs.	

8 READING Work experience in Germany ___ / 8

Text A
Hello! We are two pupils from Robert May's School in Odiham and we went on a work experience in Germany. Our work placement took place in a sports studio in Berlin and we stayed with amazing host families. Apart from the fact that we broke a cactus, we had lots of fun!

http://www.ukgermanconnection.org/cms/?location_id=1311

Text B
It was an amazing summer! In July, a group of eight pupils from the UK caught a flight from Heathrow to Düsseldorf. Little did they expect that a life-changing experience awaited them! In four weeks, they made many new friends from all over the world, saw the most interesting and beautiful places in Germany and immensely improved their language skills.

http://www.ukgermanconnection.org/cms/?location_id=570

Now tick whether the following statements are true, false or if the information is not given in the texts.

	True	False	Not given
1 The young people in text A worked in a sports shop.			
2 They got on well with their host families.			
3 They made lots of friends.			
4 They visited many different places.			
5 The young people in text B learned a lot of German.			
6 They had wonderful host families.			
7 They made lots of friends.			
8 The young people in both texts found some things surprising.			

9 WRITING The right job for me ___ / 20

Write a text of about 120–140 words about your dream job.

Think about

- the personal qualities you would need
- why you would need them
- what you would have to do in this job
- what you would like most / wouldn't like about this job
- why you think you would be the right person for this job (personal qualities)

10 WRITING A letter of application for a summer job ____ / 20

You want to apply for a summer job in England. You have found the following advert on the internet.

We want you as a **shop assistant** for our small CD and DVD shop in the town centre. We need help in the afternoons and at weekends in the summer holidays.	You love music and films and like talking to people? – Then apply and join our young team. **Send your letter of application and CV to:** The Music Shop High Street Hertford SG14 3SY

Write a letter of application for the job in the advert.
Remember to write a formal letter. Start and finish it in the correct way.

11 MEDIATION A summer job in the USA ____ / 12

You are good at tennis and want to work as an instructor for children in the next summer holidays.
You have found the following advert on the internet.

Company:	Summer Jobs
Location:	Florida
Money:	about $500 for a month and a free flight
Start:	July–August
Duration:	four to six weeks

Description:

You are good at tennis? You have experience with children?

Then show your skills by working as a tennis instructor in one of our summer camps this year.

You will teach different groups of children, 4–6 activity sessions per day.

You will also have to make the instruction plan, set up the court and ensure that the children are entertained and looked after at all times.

You will work from Monday to Friday. You will start work at 9 o'clock in the morning and finish in the afternoon.

So there is plenty of time to do some sightseeing too.

If you want to work with children, find new friends and have fun, contact us today!

Dein Großvater möchte gerne alles über diesen Sommerjob wissen. Da sein Englisch nicht gut ist, musst du ihm seine Fragen auf Deutsch beantworten.

- Wo ist die Stelle?
- Was für ein Job ist das?
- Was musst du dort machen?
- Wie lang ist die tägliche Arbeitszeit?
- Wie ist die Bezahlung?
- Was klingt gut/schlecht in der Anzeige?

12 MEDIATION   A summer job at a theme park   ___ / 16

Your e-mail friend David from Bristol is staying with you for a week in the autumn. He is telling you about his summer job at Thorpe Park.

Your mother is interested in hearing about this job too because you want to do a summer job in England next year. Her English is not very good, so you have to help.

David	I worked at Thorpe Park in my summer holidays. It was great fun and I liked it very much.
You	_____
Mother	Frag doch mal, wie lange er arbeiten musste.
You	_____
David	I had to work from 10 o'clock in the morning to 6 o'clock in the afternoon. I had to work at the weekends too because the park was very busy then.
You	_____
Mother	Hat er die ganze Zeit die gleiche Arbeit gemacht?
You	_____
David	No, I didn't. First I worked at the new roller coaster which was really scary, and then I sold burgers at one of the restaurants.
You	_____
Mother	Wie viel hat er verdient?
You	_____
David	I got £300 for four weeks.
You	_____
Mother	Das ist eine ganze Menge. Was hat ihm denn am besten gefallen?
You	_____
David	I liked the free rides best. When it wasn't too busy, we were allowed to have as many rides as we liked. That was definitely the best thing, but I didn't like talking to people who got cross because they had to wait in long queues before they could have their rides.
You	_____
Mother	Das kann ich gut verstehen. Thank you, David.
David	You're welcome.

13 WORDS Say it in English ___/ 10

Sage, dass …

1 … es dir nichts ausmacht, am Wochenende zu arbeiten. _____

_____

2 … du das Formular ausgefüllt hast. _____

3 … du gerne bereit bist, deiner Schwester zu helfen. _____

_____

4 … du früher immer aufgeregt warst, wenn du eine Arbeit schreiben musstest. _____

_____

5 … dass du Ihnen Bescheid gibst, wenn du den Job nicht möchtest. _____

_____

14 WORDS What do they do? ___/ 6

Describe what these people have to do in their jobs.

1 Vet's assistant: _____

2 Builder: _____

3 Office worker: _____

4 Nurse: _____

5 Mechanic: _____

6 Police officer: _____

15 WORDS Looking for a job ____/ 9

There are quite a few things to remember when you are looking for a job. Read the following sentences and find the right word or tick the correct box.

Step 1: For a start you can read the job _____ in the newspaper.
 a) ☐ notices
 b) ☐ displays
 c) ☐ advertisements
 d) ☐ announcements

Step 2: You have to write a letter of _____ in a formal way.

Step 3: In your CV, you write your first name, your _____, your address, and your date and place of _____.

Step 4: Mention the primary and _____ schools you went to.

Step 5: When you have done work experience, mention it and the person who can give you a _____ together with his/her _____ details.

Step 6: Don't forget to _____ your CV.
 a) ☐ enclose
 b) ☐ add
 c) ☐ recommend
 d) ☐ put in

Step 7: When you are invited to an interview, make sure you are dressed _____.

Step 8: Be prepared to tell the interviewer about your strengths and _____.

16 GRAMMAR An interview for a summer job ___ / 9

Tracy was in a shoe shop for an interview with Mr Jones, the manager.
Complete the text about the interview with the correct form of the verbs.

Tracy told Mr Jones that she _____ (go) to Cotham High School. She said that her favourite subjects _____ (be) Maths and English.

Mr Jones said that it _____ (be) useful to be good at Maths for this job and that he _____ (need) someone for the shop during the summer holidays. Tracy told Mr Jones that she _____ (know) about that. Then she told him that she _____ (have) some work experience. She said that she _____ (work) in a flower shop in the summer and she _____ (clean) at a day centre for old people.

At the end of the interview Mr Jones told her that he _____ (want) her for the job.

17 GRAMMAR The reality TV show ___ / 8

At the reality TV show Simon Gubbins gave Lucy and Mani some tips for their interview with Rita McQueen.
Write down what he said.

1 "Wear suitable clothes." – **He told them** _____

2 "Don't wear trendy clothes or jeans." – **He** _____
_____

3 "Don't sit down before you are offered a seat." – _____
_____

4 "Don't talk too much." – _____

5 "Prepare your answers before the interview." – _____
_____

6 "Don't be afraid to ask questions of your own." – _____
_____

7 "Speak clearly and confidently." – _____

8 "Thank the interviewer before leaving." – _____
_____

18 GRAMMAR At the tea shop

a) Melissa applied for a summer job as a waitress in a tea shop. She had an interview with Mrs Brown, the owner. Later Melissa tells her friend Jamie about the interview.

Look at Mrs Brown's questions and write down what Melissa tells Jamie.
Remember to use the correct tense.   ____ / 6

> 1 Which school do you go to?
> 2 What are your favourite subjects?
> 3 How many languages can you speak?
> 4 What are your hobbies?
> 5 What kind of work experience do you have?
> 6 Why do you want to work in a tea shop?

She asked me which … / She wanted to know what …

b) Melissa told Jamie that she had also asked Mrs Brown some questions.

Write down what she told him.   ____ / 6

> 1 Will I get some training before I start?
> 2 Can I wear my own clothes to work?
> 3 Do you open at the weekend?
> 4 Do I have to work on Sundays?
> 5 Is the tea shop busy on Sunday afternoons?
> 6 Am I allowed to eat some cake?

I asked her if I …

Teen world

Unit 3

Übersicht der Aufgaben

Seite	Aufgabe	Kurzbeschreibung	Kompetenz	Punkte
47/48	1 **Mark's friends**	Informationen erfassen und a) zutreffende Aussagen ankreuzen b) Multiple-Choice-Aufgaben lösen c) eine E-Mail schreiben, in der es um eine Verabredung zu einem gemeinsamen Kinobesuch geht	Hörverstehen I[1] (Nach Part C) Schreiben	7 3 20
49/50	2 **Talking it over**	Detailinformationen erfassen und a) Informationen zu bestimmten Aspekten notieren b) Notizen anfertigen c) Fragen beantworten	Hörverstehen II (Nach Part C)	14 5 10
51	3 **Teenagers and their free time**	Mithilfe einer Grafik über Jugendliche und ihre Freizeitaktivitäten sprechen	Monologisches Sprechen (Nach Part A)	20
51	4 **Voluntary work**	Mithilfe von Rollenkarten eine Diskussion über ehrenamtliche Arbeit führen	Dialogisches Sprechen (Nach Part C)	20
52/53	5 **Boot Camps**	Einen Auszug aus einem Roman lesen und a) den Absätzen Überschriften zuordnen b) die Informationen des Lesetextes in einem Artikel für ein Jugendmagazin wiedergeben	Leseverstehen I (Nach Part B) Schreiben	5 20
54/55	6 **'TXT don't talk' say young people**	a) Ein Umfrageergebnis in Form einer Grafik lesen und Aussagen Jugendlicher als typisch, untypisch oder keines von beidem klassifizieren und die Auswahl begründen b) Ein Umfrageergebnis in Form einer Grafik lesen und Aussagen Jugendlicher als typisch oder untypisch klassifizieren und die Auswahl begründen	Leseverstehen II (Nach Part A)	8 8

---

[1] Die Hörtexte zu dieser Unit wurden frei gesprochen anhand einer vorgegebenen Situation, d. h. ohne ausformulierte Textvorlage aufgenommen. Sie liegen deshalb nicht in schriftlicher Form vor.

Seite	Aufgabe	Kurzbeschreibung	Kompetenz	Punkte
56	7 **A letter to your headmaster**	Einen Brief an einen Schulleiter schreiben und die Meinung zum Thema „Verbot von Handys in der Schule" äußern	Schreiben I (Nach Part A)	20
56	8 **A written discussion**	Eine *written discussion* zu einem von drei vorgeschlagenen Themen schreiben	Schreiben II (Nach Part C)	20
57	9 **Applying for the Worldwide Voluntary Service**	Einen Bewerbungsbogen ausfüllen und in einem kurzen Text Informationen über sich selbst geben	Schreiben III (Nach Part C)	20
58	10 **How to use a cash machine**	Den Gebrauch eines Geldautomaten auf Deutsch erklären	Sprachmittlung I (Nach Part A)	10
59	11 **In a mobile phone shop**	In einem Handygeschäft in Deutschland zwischen einem Touristen und dem Verkäufer vermitteln	Sprachmittlung II (Nach Part A)	11
60	12 **Paraphrasing**	a) Umschriebene Wörter finden und aufschreiben b) Wortumschreibungen schriftlich festhalten	Wortschatz I (Nach Part A)	4 8
60	13 **Odd word out**	Einen von vier Begriffen als nicht zu den anderen passend identifizieren und die Auswahl begründen	Wortschatz II (Nach Part C)	10
61	14 **A presentation**	In einen Präsentationstext Verben im Passiv einsetzen	Grammatik (Nach Part C)	10

1 LISTENING Mark's friends 🎧 10, 🎧 11

a) Text 1 🎧 10   ___ / 7

You are going to hear some young people talking in a fast food restaurant. Jessica, Sarah and Jason are speaking about their friend Mark, who has been given an ASBO.

Look at the task, then listen to the conversation and tick the correct facts. There are five more items than you need.

Reasons for the ASBO	
1 Not going to school regularly	
2 Taking a gun to school	
3 Hanging around town	
4 Stealing things from a shop	
5 Throwing litter around	
6 Drinking alcohol	
7 Damaging a car	
8 Throwing a stone through a shop window	

Mark's ASBO

Mark isn't allowed to …	
9 … go out in the evening.	
10 … go to school clubs.	
11 … invite any friend to his house.	
12 … meet two or more friends together in town.	

b) Text 2 🎧 11   ___ / 3

Now Sarah is talking to Mark. Read the sentences below, then listen to the dialogue and tick the right statement (a, b or c).

1 Sarah	a) can't understand why Mark hung out with Adam and Tim.	
	b) wants to help Mark with the ASBO.	
	c) wants to meet Mark at the weekend.	
2 Mark	a) is angry about the ASBO.	
	b) can't do anything about the ASBO.	
	c) doesn't understand why his parents are angry about his ASBO.	
3 Mark smashed a car because	a) his friends Adam and Tim made him do it.	
	b) he read about it in a book.	
	c) he was bored.	

c) It is Saturday and Sarah is still thinking about the conversation she had with Mark. She decides to write an e-mail to him because she now thinks that she wants to go to the cinema with him.

____ / 20

Write Sarah's e-mail.

In this mail

- say why you are writing
- apologize for your reaction in the fast food restaurant
- suggest a film which you could watch together at the cinema
- suggest a place and a time to meet

Write about 130 words.

2 LISTENING Talking it over 🎧 12, 🎧 13, 🎧 14

a) Dialogue 1: Julie and Natalie 🎧 12 ____ / 14

Look at Natalie and Julie's profiles. Then listen to the dialogue and fill in the missing information.

Natalie

- Workplace:
  _____

- Thing she learns about in her job:
  _____

- Something she especially likes about her work:
  _____

- Saturday activities (Name 2.):
  _____
  _____

Julie

- Still at school
- Workplace on Saturdays:
  _____

  Activities she does with the children on Saturdays (Name 2 items.):
  _____
  _____
  _____

- Reason for enjoying her work:
  _____
  _____

Natalie and Julie are planning to meet:

Day: _____ Time: _____

Place: _____

Things they will do together (Name 2 items.): _____,
_____

---

b) Dialogue 2: Jack and Melanie 🎧 13 ____ / 5

Listen to the conversation between Jack and Melanie and make some notes in the table below.

Things Jack suggests the two could do together (Name 3 items.)	Reasons why Melanie does not want to go out with Jack (Name 2 items.)

c) *Dialogue 3: Laura and Hannah* 🎧 14 ____/ 10

Listen to the conversation between Laura and Hannah about Laura's birthday party and answer the questions below in 1–5 words or numbers.

1 When is Laura's birthday party?	
2 How many guests does she want to invite to her party?	
3 What food are the girls planning to have at the party? (Name two.)	1 _____ 2 _____
4 What present does Laura want from her parents?	
5 What's special about this present?	Colour: _____ Functions: 1 _____ 2 _____
6 What does Hannah think about this present? (Name two things.)	1 _____ 2 _____

3 SPEAKING Teenagers and their free time ____ / 20

Look at the chart on teenagers and their free-time activities below. Prepare a talk of about three minutes. You've got ten minutes to prepare it.

Talk about

– the chart and what it shows you
– your favourite free-time activities

Do you think the chart would look the same if you and your friends had been asked? What would be different?

Do you think that it is a problem that teenagers spend a lot of time using modern technology instead of doing other activities?

Yesterday, did you …

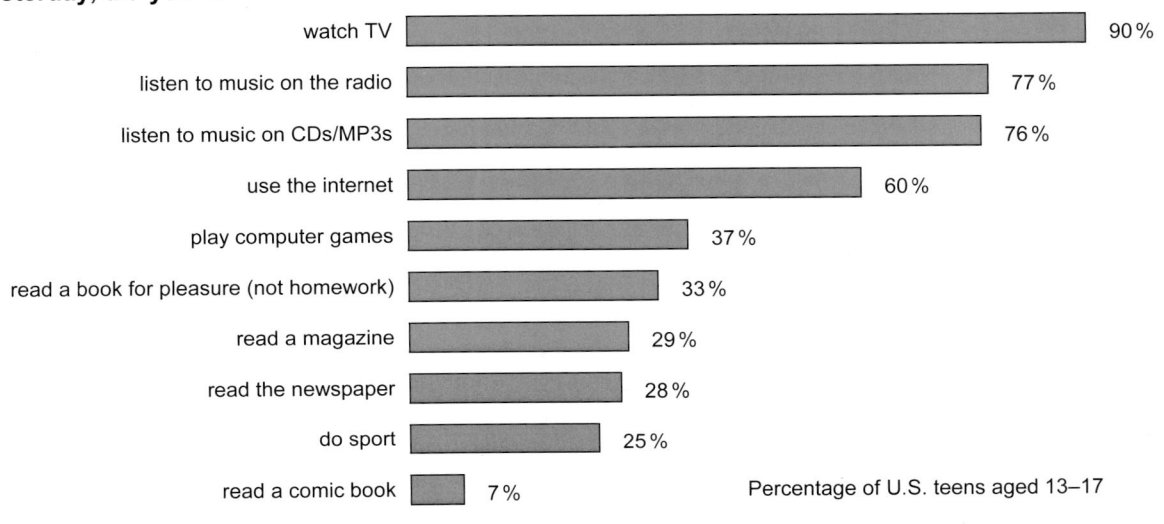

Activity	Percentage
watch TV	90%
listen to music on the radio	77%
listen to music on CDs/MP3s	76%
use the internet	60%
play computer games	37%
read a book for pleasure (not homework)	33%
read a magazine	29%
read the newspaper	28%
do sport	25%
read a comic book	7%

Percentage of U.S. teens aged 13–17

http://media.gallup.com/GPTB/educaYouth/20041026_1.gif

4 SPEAKING Voluntary work ____ / 20

You are in England on an exchange visit. You've just watched a documentary about voluntary work with your exchange partner.

Prepare a dialogue of about three minutes. You've got ten minutes to prepare it.

Discuss with your partner. Remember to use discussion phrases.

Partner A

You are an English teenager. At the moment a German exchange student is staying with you. You have just watched a documentary about voluntary work together with your exchange partner.
You would like to do some voluntary work in your free time. Here are some of your reasons:

- meet people
- do something good
- get work experience for later
- …

Partner B

You are in England on an exchange visit. You have just watched a documentary about voluntary work together with your exchange partner.
You don't want to do voluntary work in your free time. Here are some of your reasons:

- not much free time
- not get paid for it
- want to do something relaxing in your free time
- …

5 READING Boot Camps

In the middle of the night Garrett is taken from his home to Harmony Lake, a boot camp for troubled teens. Maybe some kids deserve to be there, but Garrett knows he doesn't. Subjected[1] to brutal physical and psychological abuse[2], he tries to fight back, but the battle is futile[3]. He won't be allowed to leave until he's admitted his "mistakes" …

From the cover of *Boot Camp* by Todd Strasser

A secret prison system for teenagers exists in the United States. Many have never heard of it, and even among those who have, few understand what it really is or how it works. You do not have to be found guilty of a crime to be placed in one of these prisons, also known as boot camps. You do not even have to be accused of committing a crime. All you have to do is be under the age of eighteen.

It is impossible to know how many boot camps exist. Estimates put the number between one hundred and two hundred, and the number of teens in them between four thousand and ten thousand. Most boot camps avoid publicity, preferring instead to advertise their services privately and by word of mouth. In addition a number of boot camps have been set up outside United States borders – especially in Central America and the Caribbean, but also as far away as Thailand and the Philippines – to avoid American regulations against the mistreatment[4] of teenage detainees. […]

Once in a boot camp, teens are cut off from the outside world. They are not allowed to communicate with anyone except their parents, who are warned in advance that complaints of physical abuse and maltreatment are lies – attempts by their child to "manipulate" them in order to be taken out of the boot camp. All forms of news and current entertainment are forbidden in order to reinforce the impression that the world inside the boot camp is the only thing that matters.

At the age of eighteen, teens are legally considered adults and therefore allowed to leave the facility if they choose. But teens under the age of eighteen have no choice. Should parents decide for any reason that they've had enough of a child, they can sentence him or her to boot camp. And the child is helpless to stop them.

Todd Strasser: *Boot Camp* – Afterword

---

[1] (to) be subjected to sth. *etw. ausgesetzt sein*
[2] abuse *Missbrauch*
[3] futile *vergeblich, sinnlos*
[4] mistreatment *Misshandlung*

a) *The text can be divided into the following parts:* _____/ 5

Lines 1–4   ☐

Lines 6–9   ☐

Lines 10–15 ☐

Lines 16–20 ☐

Lines 21–24 ☐

Match the given parts with the correct heading and write the letter into the box next to the lines above. There is one more heading than you need.

A What a boot camp is
B Facts and figures
C A personal story
D Life in a boot camp
E How to protest against boot camp
F No rights for the Under-18s

b) *Imagine you spent six months in such a boot camp. Write an article for a teen magazine in which you describe your life there.* _____/ 20

Write
- what your day was like
- how you were treated
- whether your life has changed after your stay
- …

6 READING 'TXT don't talk' say young people

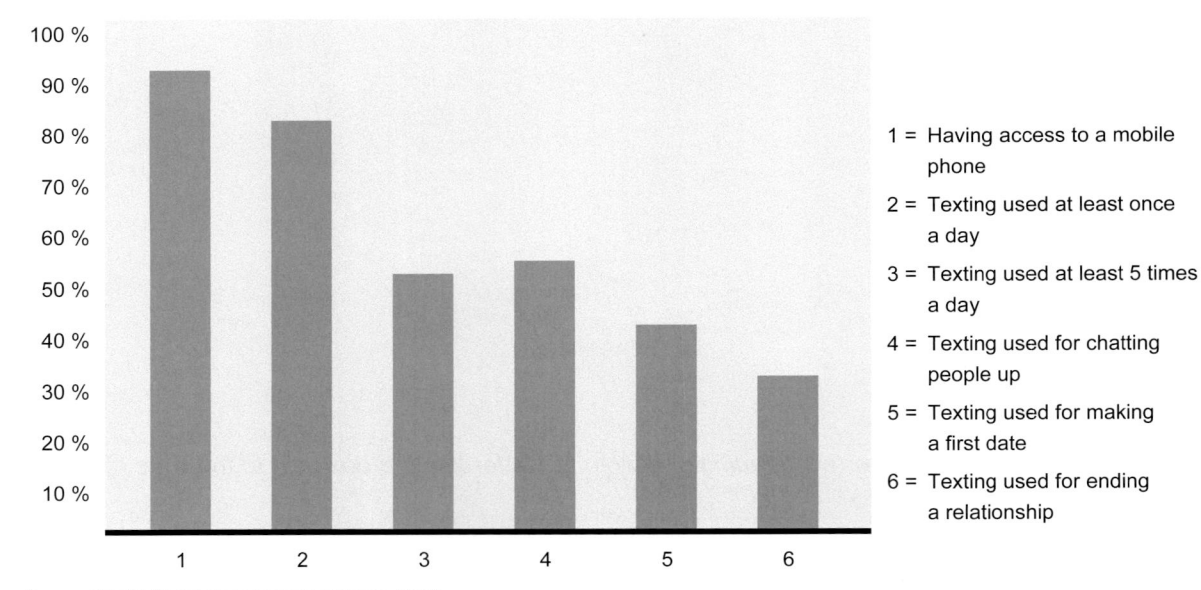

a) Look at the results of a survey on young people and texting with their mobiles: _____ / 8

1 = Having access to a mobile phone
2 = Texting used at least once a day
3 = Texting used at least 5 times a day
4 = Texting used for chatting people up
5 = Texting used for making a first date
6 = Texting used for ending a relationship

Source: Nestlé Social Research Programme, 2004

Read the following statements made by young people, underline the correct answer (typical, not typical, neither [weder ... noch]), and say why.

Sarah: "Well, I see my friends at school and can talk to them there. I only use my mobile at weekends when I'm out and need to tell my parents where I am and when I'll be home – and if I need them to fetch me because I've missed the bus. But I always ring them, as I know they're at home."

Typical / Not typical / Neither because _____

_____

Mark: "I live on a farm out in the country, and I need to be able to communicate with my mates. Of course, we see each other at school, but you can't really talk there, so afternoons and evenings we text each other all the time."

Typical / Not typical / Neither because _____

_____

Nadja: "When I finished with my last boyfriend, I had to tell him to his face. Of course, it would have been easier to text him, but I didn't think that was fair, so I asked him to meet me and told him. It was hard, but I thought it was best."

Typical / Not typical / Neither because _____

_____

Tom: "If I want to go out with a girl, I always text her. I wouldn't want to be given a 'no' to my face, would I?"

Typical / Not typical / Neither because _____

_____

b) Using a mobile in public: _____ / 8

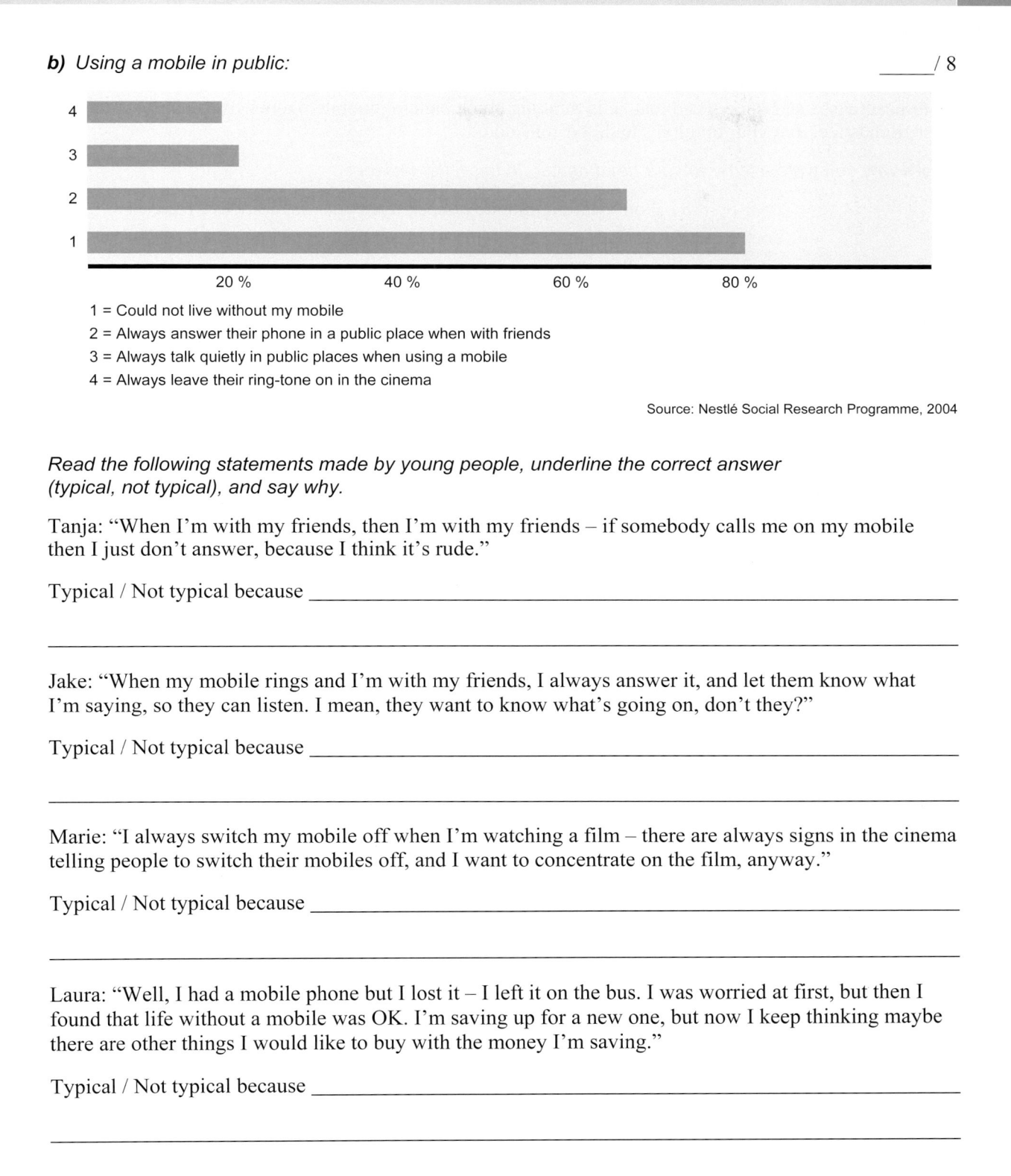

```
4 ▆▆▆▆
3 ▆▆▆▆▆
2 ▆▆▆▆▆▆▆▆▆▆▆▆▆▆▆▆
1 ▆▆▆▆▆▆▆▆▆▆▆▆▆▆▆▆▆▆▆▆
   20 %    40 %    60 %    80 %
```

1 = Could not live without my mobile
2 = Always answer their phone in a public place when with friends
3 = Always talk quietly in public places when using a mobile
4 = Always leave their ring-tone on in the cinema

Source: Nestlé Social Research Programme, 2004

Read the following statements made by young people, underline the correct answer (typical, not typical), and say why.

Tanja: "When I'm with my friends, then I'm with my friends – if somebody calls me on my mobile then I just don't answer, because I think it's rude."

Typical / Not typical because _____

_____

Jake: "When my mobile rings and I'm with my friends, I always answer it, and let them know what I'm saying, so they can listen. I mean, they want to know what's going on, don't they?"

Typical / Not typical because _____

_____

Marie: "I always switch my mobile off when I'm watching a film – there are always signs in the cinema telling people to switch their mobiles off, and I want to concentrate on the film, anyway."

Typical / Not typical because _____

_____

Laura: "Well, I had a mobile phone but I lost it – I left it on the bus. I was worried at first, but then I found that life without a mobile was OK. I'm saving up for a new one, but now I keep thinking maybe there are other things I would like to buy with the money I'm saving."

Typical / Not typical because _____

_____

7 WRITING   A letter to your headmaster   ___ / 20

Your headmaster has announced that he is thinking about banning mobile phones from school. You and your friends feel that your opinion should be considered.

That's why you write a letter to your headmaster. In this letter include:

- Your opinion about banning mobile phones from your school. Give reasons.
- Your experiences with mobile phones at school. Are there any problems?
- A solution or a compromise

Write your text in about 150 words. Remember that this is a formal letter.

You may use the information given in the newspaper article below.

Mobiles at school: to ban or not to ban?

More and more schools have started banning mobile phones from their classrooms. Some schools don't even let their students take them into the school building. The reasons are not obvious to everyone.

Parents in particular often don't see why their child is not allowed to take a mobile to school. "My son George needs to take it with him," says Tracy Bradford, a concerned single mother. "What if I need to talk to him? Sometimes we have to make arrangements during the day and therefore he needs a phone." Another argument the opponents often raise are cases of emergency in which students can easily call for help with their mobile phones.

"These arguments have all been taken into account," Michael Redcap explains. "If students are in the school building and there is an emergency, there will always be a phone nearby. However, recent incidents show that mobile phones promote a wide range of anti-social behaviour that we cannot tolerate. Cameras in phones are used to film teachers or other students. These short video clips often end up on the internet without the person knowing. Very often this leads to mobile phone bullying. Sometimes those videos show embarrassing situations."

The supporters of the ban also state that there have been numerous cases in which mobile phones were used to cheat in exams.

8 WRITING   A written discussion   ___ / 20

Collect ideas for or against one of the statements below:

Boot camps should be introduced for troublemakers in Germany.

Voluntary work should be compulsory for everyone.

ASBOs should be introduced in Germany.

Then write a written discussion of about 150 words. Remember to use the following structure for your text:

- Introduction to the topic
- Arguments for or against
- Conclusion

9 WRITING Applying for the Worldwide Voluntary Service   ____ / 20

You want to take part in the WWVS (Worldwide Voluntary Service) scheme. They sent you the application form below. Fill in the form and write your personal summary (of about 100 words) on a separate piece of paper.

The Worldwide Voluntary Service

Who we are:
The WWVS is an organization based in Brussels, Belgium. We offer voluntary services to young people aged 16–25 and have partner organizations all over the world, so no matter where you want to do your service – in North America, Africa or elsewhere in the world – the WWVS provides you with work that suits your personality. Our placements range from working with old, young and disabled people to working in community centres, churches, shelters for the homeless and many more.

Taking part in our scheme will be a unique experience and will change the way you look at life. Our volunteers are provided with pocket money and accommodation for the time of their stay.

The Worldwide Voluntary Service Application

Full name: _____

Date of birth: _____   Sex: _____

Nationality: _____

Address: _____

Preferred country for service: _____

Preferred type of work: _____

Personal summary
Write a paragraph about yourself: why you want to take part in the scheme, personal/practical skills, experience, what you think is hard about taking part in the WWVS scheme, which type of work you would like to do.

Use a separate piece of paper.

10 MEDIATION   How to use a cash machine   ___ / 10

You have just arrived at Heathrow Airport in London with your parents. They need to get some money from a cash machine.

Deine Eltern können nur wenig Englisch. Erkläre ihnen die einzelnen Schritte, die nötig sind, um Geld aus dem Automaten zu bekommen.

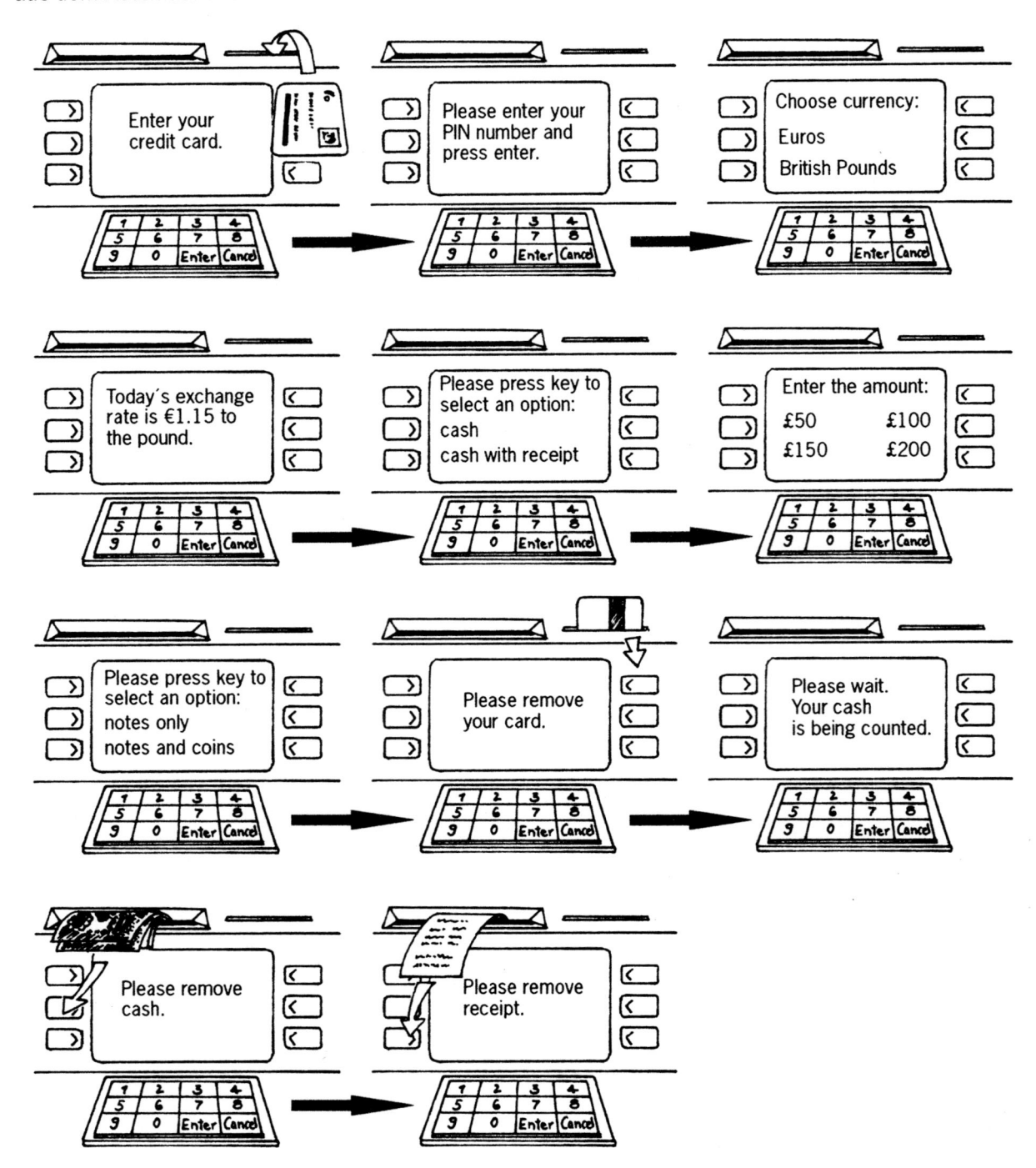

Screen 1: Enter your credit card.
Screen 2: Please enter your PIN number and press enter.
Screen 3: Choose currency: Euros / British Pounds
Screen 4: Today's exchange rate is €1.15 to the pound.
Screen 5: Please press key to select an option: cash / cash with receipt
Screen 6: Enter the amount: £50 £100 £150 £200
Screen 7: Please press key to select an option: notes only / notes and coins
Screen 8: Please remove your card.
Screen 9: Please wait. Your cash is being counted.
Screen 10: Please remove cash.
Screen 11: Please remove receipt.

0   Als erstes müsst ihr die Kreditkarte in den Geldautomaten stecken.
1   …

11 MEDIATION   In a mobile phone shop   ____ / 11

Your American friend Paul is with you in Germany. You are in a mobile phone shop because Paul needs a mobile phone. Help him and the shop assistant understand each other.

Shop assistant   Hallo. Kann ich Ihnen helfen?

You   Ja, mein Freund möchte ein neues Handy kaufen. Ihm gefällt das hier sehr gut. Wir würden es uns gerne noch einmal genau ansehen.

Shop assistant   Hier, bitte schön.

Paul   How much is the phone?

You   Können Sie uns sagen, was das Handy kostet?

Shop assistant   Es kostet € 99,90.

You   _____

Paul   Is the phone blocked?

You   _____

Shop assistant   Nein, ist es nicht. Sie können also Ihre alte SIM-Karte benutzen oder eine neue.

You   _____

Paul   OK, I would like to buy it then. Could you ask if I can pay by credit card?

You   _____
_____

Shop assistant   Natürlich.

You   _____

Shop assistant   Sie müssen auf jeden Fall den Kassenbon aufbewahren.

You   _____

Paul   Can I just start using the phone now? I have my SIM-card here.

You   _____

Shop assistant   Ja, aber Sie müssen zuerst Ihre Geheimzahl eingeben.

You   _____

Paul   OK, let's go then.

You   Danke. Auf Wiedersehen.

12 WORDS   Paraphrasing

a) *Write down the word that is described in the sentence.* ____ / 4

1 It wakes you up in the morning: _____

2 Having a lot of things to do. Being _____

3 You get this when you buy something. It says what you bought and how much you paid: _____

4 When nobody knows that you did something you did it _____

b) *Now write definitions for these words:* ____ / 8

1 only child: _____

2 face-to-face: _____

3 (to) ban: _____

4 cash: _____

13 WORDS   Odd word out   ____ / 10

Find the odd word out and underline it. Then explain why you think it is the odd word out.

1 (to) shoplift – (to) punish – (to) threaten – (to) vandalize
_____

2 can – coin – note – bill
_____

3 river – lake – trash – spring
_____

4 receipt – court – cash – exchange rate
_____

5 wedding – funeral – birthday – behaviour
_____

14 GRAMMAR A presentation ___/ 10

Read the text. It is part of a presentation some young people gave on a voluntary project their school supported. Fill in the gaps using the passive.

As you all know our school is collecting money for a voluntary project in Tanzania.

First of all: thanks to all of you. A lot of money _____ (collect) over the last six months to support the volunteers' work.

Today we would like to tell you what _____ (do) so far in the Tanzanian village:

The new school building _____ (finish).

Toilets and showers _____ (built).

The street leading to the school _____ (repair).

Two school buses _____ (buy).

Plans for the coming months:

New school books _____ (must – buy).

A computer _____ (must – install).

Trees _____ (will – plant) around the school.

English and Maths teachers _____ (must – find).

Thank you for your attention.

Unit 4 Exploring cities

Übersicht der Aufgaben

Seite	Aufgabe	Kurzbeschreibung	Kompetenz	Punkte
64	1 **Movie talk**	Informationen erfassen und Notizen in eine Tabelle eintragen bzw. die richtige Spalte ankreuzen	Hörverstehen I[1] (Nach Part A)	22
65/66	2 **Getting to places**	Informationen erfassen und a) Fragen in Stichworten beantworten b) Fragen in Stichworten beantworten c) eine Multiple-Choice Aufgabe lösen	Hörverstehen II (Nach Part C)	12 8 5
67	3 **Talking about photos**	Über ein Foto sprechen	Monologisches Sprechen (Nach Part B)	20
68	4 **At the doctor's**	Mithilfe von Rollenkarten ein Patienten-/Arzt-Gespräch führen	Dialogisches Sprechen (Nach Part A)	20
69/70	5 **A weekend in Berlin**	Fünf Internetbeiträge lesen und a) den richtigen Zeitplan ankreuzen b) fehlerhafte Informationen in den übrigen vier Zeitplänen unterstreichen	Leseverstehen I (Nach Part C)	1 4
71/72	6 **Nelson Mandela**	Einen Text über Nelson Mandela lesen und eine Multiple-Choice-Aufgabe lösen	Leseverstehen II (Nach Part C)	10
73	7 **Life in big cities**	Seine Meinung zum Leben in einer Großstadt äußern	Schreiben I (Nach Part B)	20
73	8 **My impressions of Mumbai and Johannesburg**	In einem strukturierten Text seine gewonnenen Eindrücke zu Mumbai und Johannesburg schildern	Schreiben II (Nach Part B)	20
73	9 **Berlin – a great place to stay**	Eine E-Mail an die Partnerschule in England schreiben und darin über eine gemeinsam geplante Berlinfahrt informieren	Schreiben III (Nach Part C)	20

[1] Die Transkripte der Hörtexte zu dieser Unit finden Sie als kostenloses Online-Angebot auf unserer Website **www.englishg.de** unter >Downloads<.

Seite	Aufgabe	Kurzbeschreibung	Kompetenz	Punkte
74	10 **Histmarol Cream**	Den Inhalt eines Beipackzettels auf Deutsch erklären	Sprachmittlung I (Nach Part A)	12
75	11 **At a youth hostel in Berlin**	In einer zweisprachigen Situation vermitteln	Sprachmittlung II (Nach Part C)	16
76	12 **Words in combination I**	a) Wortpaare bilden aus Verb, Adjektiv und Substantiv b) mit ausgewählten Wortpaaren einen sinnvollen Satz bilden	Wortschatz I (Nach Part A)	6 3
76	13 **Words in combination II**	a) Verben/Adjektive mit passender Präposition kombinieren b) Sätze mit passenden Wortpaaren ergänzen	Wortschatz II (Nach Part C)	5 5
77	14 **Find the right words**	Wörter finden	Wortschatz III (Nach Part C)	11
78	15 **What if …?**	a) Conditional-Sätze Typ 1, 2 und 3 verstehen und das richtige Bild ankreuzen b) Conditional-Sätze Typ 3 verstehen und den richtigen Hauptsatz ankreuzen	Grammatik I (Nach Part C)	2 (je 0,5) 2 (je 0,5)
79	16 **I would have stayed at home**	In Minidialogen schreiben, wie man anstelle des Gesprächspartners gehandelt hätte	Grammatik II (Nach Part C)	5

1 LISTENING Movie talk 🎧 15   ____ / 22

Listen to two young people talking about a film and complete the table below.
Some of the information in the table has been completed for you. You will hear the recording twice.

	Boy's film	Girl's film
1 Watched – when?	night before	
2 Hero		
3 Nationality		
4 Set in which country?		
5 Which channel?		
The Plot *Tick the boy's film, the girl's film or both films.*		
6 The guy works in a call centre.	☐	☐
7 The guy falls in love with an Indian girl.	☐	☐
8 The guy wins a lot of money.	☐	☐
9 The call centre is in an empty garage.	☐	☐
10 The guy gets arrested.	☐	☐
11 The guy teaches English.	☐	☐
12 The guy grew up in a poor neighbourhood.	☐	☐
13 Mood	No information	1 _____ 2 _____
14 Happy ending? Yes? No? Don't know?		

2 LISTENING Getting to places 🎧 16, 🎧 17, 🎧 18

a) Dialogue 1 🎧 16   ____ / 12

Listen to the dialogue and answer the following questions in 1–5 words or numbers.
You will hear the recording twice.

1 Where does the couple have a stopover?	
2 How long is the stopover?	From _____ to _____.
3 How can they get into the city centre?	
4 What can they see from the Peak? (Name 2 things.)	1 _____ 2 _____
5 How can they get there? (Name 2 means of transport.)	1 _____ 2 _____
6 What can they do in the afternoon? (Name 3 activities.)	1 _____ 2 _____ 3 _____
7 What does the couple think of the assistant's advice?	

b) Dialogue 2 🎧 17 ___/ 8

*Listen to the dialogue and answer the following questions in 1–5 words or numbers.
You will hear the recording twice.*

1 When does the man arrive?	
2 Where does his plane land?	
3 What's the best way to get from the airport to the hotel?	
4 How long will it take?	
5 How much does it cost?	
6 How can he get to the Kurfürstendamm?	
7 How can he get to the Reichstag? (Name two means of transport.)	1 _____ 2 _____

c) Dialogue 3 🎧 18 ___/ 5

Listen to the dialogue and tick the correct answer a, b, c or d. You will hear the recording once.

1 The woman calls	a) to book a flight to Frankfurt.	
	b) to ask about flight details.	
	c) to cancel [stornieren] her flight.	
	d) to change her flight times.	
2 The flight number is	a) AE 191.	
	b) IE 191.	
	c) AI 191.	
	d) EA 191.	
3 The plane departs at	a) 1:45 am.	
	b) 1:54 am.	
	c) 1:45 pm.	
	d) 1:55 am.	
4 The plane arrives in Frankfurt at	a) 6:30 pm.	
	b) 6:13 pm.	
	c) 6:30 am.	
	d) 6:13 am.	
5 The woman should come to the check-in in Mumbai	a) not earlier than three hours before departure.	
	b) at least two hours before departure.	
	c) three hours before departure or earlier.	
	d) exactly three hours before departure.	

4

3 SPEAKING Talking about photos   ____ / 20

Pupil A

Look at the photo and the task. Describe the photo in a detailed way. Imagine you're describing it to someone who can't see it. Talk about the photo for about two to three minutes. You've got ten minutes to prepare your talk.

Talk about:
- the situation
- the place
- the time of day
- the things you can see
- the people and what they are doing

Talk about what you feel, 'hear' etc. when you look at this picture.

Would you like to go on holiday there or even live there for a time? Say why or why not.

Pupil B

Look at the photo and the task. Describe the photo in a detailed way. Imagine you're describing it to someone who can't see it. Talk about the photo for about two to three minutes. You've got ten minutes to prepare your talk.

Talk about:
- the situation
- the place
- the time of day
- the things you can see
- the people and what they are doing

Speculate on why the people are in the street and what their aim is. Talk about what you feel, 'hear' etc. when you look at this picture. Would you like to be with the people? Say why or why not.

4 SPEAKING At the doctor's

_____ / 20

a) Look at the role cards and prepare a dialogue of about two minutes.
You've got ten minutes to prepare it.

Partner A

You've been ill for two days with a terrible cough, a sore throat and a temperature (39 °C).
Your whole body is aching.

You go and see the doctor (Partner B).

Start and finish your dialogue in a friendly way.

Partner B

A patient who doesn't feel well (Partner A) comes to see you.

- Ask what the matter is and examine him/her.
- Prescribe some medicine.
- Give some advice:
  – stay in bed
  – come back in three days
  – drink lots of …

Start and finish your dialogue in a friendly way.

OR

b) Look at the role cards and prepare a dialogue of about two minutes.
You've got ten minutes to prepare it.

Partner A

You've been sick for three days with a stomach ache. You go and see the doctor (Partner B).

Start and finish your dialogue in a friendly way.

Partner B

A patient who has been sick (Partner A) comes to see you.

- Ask him/her:
  – how long
  – about the food he/she has eaten
  – about drinks
- Prescribe:
  – medicine, capsules, drops
- Suggest:
  – lots of tea, mineral water
  – no coffee
  – a special diet for the next three days

Come again – three days – appointment necessary

Start and finish your dialogue in a friendly way.

5 Reading A weekend in Berlin

Two British teenagers have posted a message on a website asking for information about things to do as a tourist in Berlin. They've already received six answers.

We're visiting Berlin next month for a long weekend. We've only got two days, but we want to see as much as we can. Any suggestions?

Sarah and James

Two days aren't enough for Berlin – there's so much to do! Start with a walking tour. The tours are in English and they leave every morning at 10 am from Hackescher Markt. Don't forget your walking shoes! If it's raining or you don't like walking, go on a bus tour instead.

Angela

The shops in Berlin are awesome – there are huge shopping centers and small boutiques. We spent hours shopping in "Prenzlauer Berg" and bought lots of clothes by designers you can't find in the States. Our friends were sooooo jealous when we got back home.

Zach

Zach's right, the shops in Berlin are great. But they aren't open on Sundays – you've been warned! When you've finished with the shops, you can visit one of Berlin's cafés just like the locals. The cakes at Schulz's in Mitte are delicious. My other tip is to remember to take some sunscreen and a hat with you – Berlin can be very HOT in summer.

Julia

We went to Berlin on a school history trip last year. We visited some really interesting sights and museums. My favourite was the Jewish Museum. We learned all about the history of the Jews in Germany and in Europe. The museum is very big, so plan a whole morning or afternoon. I was also very impressed by the Reichstag – and it's free to visit! Have a great time!

Tim

Sarah and James have read the advice on the forum and have made some plans for the weekend.

a) Which plan follows all the advice they were given? Tick A, B, C, D or E.   ____ / 1

b) Underline the parts of the other plans which are wrong.   ____ / 4

A
Friday evening – arrive in Berlin and check into hostel
Saturday am – walking tour of Berlin
pm – visit the Jewish Museum
Sunday am – visit the Reichstag
pm – shopping in Prenzlauer Berg, break in a café
evening – flight back to London

B
Friday evening – arrive in Berlin and check into hostel
Saturday am – shopping!
pm – a break in a café
Sunday am – walking tour of Berlin
pm – visit the Jewish Museum and the Reichstag
evening – flight back to London

C
Friday evening – arrive in Berlin and check into hostel
Saturday am – walking tour of Berlin
pm – shopping in Prenzlauer Berg, break in a café
Sunday am – visit the Jewish Museum
pm – visit the Reichstag
evening – flight back to London

D
Friday evening – arrive in Berlin and check into hostel
Saturday am – shopping in Prenzlauer Berg
pm – walking tour of Berlin
Sunday am – visit the Jewish Museum
pm – visit the Reichstag
evening – flight back to London

E
Friday evening – arrive in Berlin and check into hostel
Saturday am – visit the Jewish Museum
pm – shopping in Prenzlauer Berg, break in a café
Sunday am – visit the Reichstag
pm – walking tour of Berlin
evening – flight back to London

6 READING Nelson Mandela   ___ / 10

Nelson Mandela was President of South Africa from 1994 until 1999. He was the first South African President to be elected in democratic elections by the whole South African population. Until 1994 black South Africans were not allowed to vote.

5 Today, Nelson Mandela is a legend. He is loved and respected by millions of people in South Africa and all over the world. However, during apartheid, for many white South Africans he was a terrorist. Mandela spent twenty-seven years in prison for his role in the anti-apartheid movement. He was the leader of the African National Congress (ANC). The ANC
10 believed that all people should have the same rights and opportunities whatever the colour of their skin. They said that apartheid was wrong. The apartheid government sometimes reacted violently when black South Africans demonstrated.

In the 1950s the ANC's protests were non-violent, but the situation of black South Africans did not
15 improve. In 1961 Mandela and other ANC members started to organize attacks on government and military buildings. They felt that violence was the only way to change the situation in their country.

Mandela was sent to prison in 1962. When he was in prison, he became a symbol of the fight against apartheid. He had many supporters not just in South Africa. Life was very hard for the prisoners. Mandela's cell was just 5m². Prisoners had to sleep on a very thin mattress on a stone floor and he had
20 to work long hours outside every day. He did not have suitable clothes. He was allowed very few visitors and not many letters. Although everyday life was difficult, Mandela continued to study.

In 1989 Frederik Willem de Klerk became President of South Africa. In February 1990 de Klerk announced that Nelson Mandela would be let out of prison. On 11 February 1990, the moment Mandela walked free was shown on television stations in countries all over the world. That day Mandela made a
25 speech to the nation. He said the ANC had reacted with violence against the violence of apartheid. He hoped that the situation in the country would change and that the South African government would give black citizens the right to vote.

In 1994 that hope became a reality and 62 per cent of South Africans voted for Nelson Mandela in the elections of April that year. There were still many serious problems in the country, but a new South
30 Africa had been born.

Complete the sentences. Tick the correct box.

1 Today many people all over the world	a) think Nelson Mandela is a hero.	
	b) think Nelson Mandela is a terrorist.	
	c) think Nelson Mandela is President of South Africa.	
2 Up until 1994 the ANC	a) was happy with the situation in South Africa.	
	b) wanted apartheid to end.	
	c) was led by was Frederik Willem de Klerk.	
3 The apartheid government	a) was popular with the ANC.	
	b) sometimes became violent when people demonstrated.	
	c) wanted black people to vote.	

4 In 1961 the ANC started to use violence because	a) they wanted the political system in South Africa to change.	
	b) they thought that apartheid should continue.	
	c) they wanted Nelson Mandela to be President of South Africa.	
5 Nelson Mandela was sent to prison because	a) he was a member of the ANC.	
	b) he was black.	
	c) he helped organize violent attacks in South Africa.	
6 When Nelson Mandela was in prison,	a) he wrote lots of letters.	
	b) people forgot about him.	
	c) life was very hard for him but he continued to read and study in his free time.	
7 President Frederik Willem de Klerk	a) respected Nelson Mandela.	
	b) said that Nelson Mandela could leave prison.	
	c) did not want elections in South Africa.	
8 When Nelson Mandela left prison,	a) the world's media was interested.	
	b) no one noticed.	
	c) there were elections in South Africa.	
9 The first democratic elections for all South Africans	a) took place in 1962.	
	b) took place in 1994.	
	c) were very violent.	
10 In 1994 Nelson Mandela was elected	a) the first President of South Africa.	
	b) the first leader of the ANC.	
	c) the first black President of South Africa.	

7 WRITING Life in big cities _____/ 20

Big cities like Mumbai, Johannesburg and Berlin are very attractive to tourists, but would you like to live in a big city?

Write a structured text of about 180 words answering this question.
Think about the positive and negative aspects of living in a big city.
Give reasons for your answer.

8 WRITING My impressions of Mumbai and Johannesburg _____/ 20

During the last few weeks you have learned a lot about Mumbai and Johannesburg – two impressive cities, two cities of contrast.

Write a structured text of about 150 words on your impressions of Mumbai or Johannesburg.

Think about

- what you personally think of Mumbai or Johannesburg
- what was most interesting, fascinating or surprising for you
- what astonished or shocked you or made you sad

Would you like to visit one or both cities one day? Why / Why not?

9 WRITING Berlin – a great place to stay _____/ 20

Imagine a group of students from your twin school is going to visit your school for one week.
Your class has planned to go on a two-day trip to Berlin with them.

Write an e-mail of 150–180 words to tell them about the trip to Berlin.

Write about

- the time of the trip
- how you are going to get there
- where you are going to stay
- 2–3 general facts about the city
- the activities planned (morning/afternoon/evening)

Start and finish your e-mail in a friendly way.

10 MEDIATION Histmarol Cream   ____ / 12

Stell dir vor, du bist mit deiner Familie in Johannesburg. Deine kleine Schwester ist von einem Insekt gebissen worden und ihr Bein ist entzündet und tut ihr sehr weh. Ein Apotheker hat euch Histmarol Cream gegeben.

Lies den Beipackzettel und informiere deine Eltern über die Angaben darin.

1 Bei welchen Verletzungen man die Salbe anwenden kann: (2)

_____

_____

2 Wie du die Salbe anwenden musst: (3)

_____

_____

3 Wann du die Salbe nicht anwenden darfst: (2)

_____

_____

4 Wie man die Salbe aufbewahren muss: (2)

_____

_____

5 Was du unbedingt bei der Anwendung beachten musst: (3)

_____

_____

_____

Histmarol Cream
If you do not understand any of the details in this leaflet, then ask your pharmacist or doctor.

What the cream is for: This medicine is for minor irritation of the skin, especially after insect bites.

Usage: For external use only. Do not use more than twice daily or for longer than five days.

When not to use the cream: Do not use on broken skin. Do not use this product if you are allergic to antihistamines.

Storage: Store between 4°C and 25°C. Keep away from children!

Special warnings: Keep away from the eyes, nose and mouth. Not suitable for children under six years of age. If the pain continues or if it occurs with a high temperature, ask a doctor right away.

11 MEDIATION At a youth hostel in Berlin ___ / 16

You're at a youth hostel in Berlin. Two young Americans are standing next to you at the reception. The receptionist's English is not very good, and so they have problems to understand him.

Help the two Americans.

You	Hello, maybe I can help you.
American	Oh great, you speak English. We're looking for somewhere to stay for a week. A room with two beds would be fine.
You	_____ (2)
Receptionist	Das ist etwas schwierig. Leider habe ich erst morgen ein Doppelzimmer. Für heute kann ich euch zwei Betten im Schlafsaal anbieten.
You	_____ (2)
American	Great. Thank you. We'll take them. How much is it and is breakfast included?
You	_____ (2)
Receptionist	Die Übernachtung im Schlafsaal kostet 10 Euro pro Nacht pro Person und das Doppelzimmer 15 Euro. Frühstück ist inbegriffen. Frühstück ist zwischen 7 und 10 Uhr.
You	_____ (4)
American	OK and where can we have a shower?
You	_____ (1)
Receptionist	Toiletten und Duschen sind im Kellergeschoss.
You	_____ (1)
American	OK.
Receptionist	Sie möchten bitte beide das Formular ausfüllen und unten unterschreiben.
You	_____ (2)
American	OK, here you are.
Receptionist	Danke. Hier ist der Schlüssel für den Schlafsaal am Ende des Flurs.
You	_____ (2)
American	Fine. Thanks a lot for your help.

12 WORDS Words in combination I

a) Which of the words go together? Write down phrases. Sometimes you have to add **a** or **an**.
Use each word only once. ____ / 6

| discover • eat at • get • know • like • speak • wear | **+** | colourful • fashionable • financial • glamorous • official • polluted • tight | **+** | clothes • help • jeans • lake • language • movie star • restaurant |

Example:

(to) like tight jeans

b) Now use three combinations and write meaningful sentences. ____ / 3

Example:

I really like tight jeans.

13 WORDS Words in combination II

a) Match the words from box 1 to the right preposition from box 2 and write them down.
Be careful. You have to use some of the prepositions more than once. ____ / 5

| **1** (to) adjust • (to) be familiar • (to) connect • (to) draw sb.'s attention • (to) give a talk • (to) hold • (to) lean • (to) live • on top • typical | **+** | **2** of • on • out • to • with |

b) Complete the sentences with suitable phrases from a). ____ / 5

1 In India, poor families have to _____ less than $30 a month.

2 When you are _____ a mountain, you've got a fantastic view.

3 Don't _____ of the window – it's dangerous.

4 When you enter a dark room, your eyes have to _____ the darkness.

5 I need your help. Are you _____ this gadget?

14 WORDS Find the right words   ____/ 11

Write down the right words.

1 the situation of having no job: _____

2 an area outside the town where people live: _____

3 the noun to the adjective "free": _____

4 the noun to the verb "(to) survive": _____

5 a large room with many beds: _____

6 a strong belief in sth.: _____

7 a very small building in a slum: _____

8 (to) break sth. into parts; (to) divide into parts: _____

9 sth. that you'll never forget is _____

10 the noun to the adjective "poor": _____

11 You can leave it on an answering machine: _____

15 GRAMMAR What if …?

a) Look at the pictures and tick the right answer. ___/ 2

If you stay a bit longer, we'll finish our presentation for tomorrow.

1 Can they finish their presentation?
　Yes ☐　　No ☐

If Tom had stayed longer, we would have finished our presentation.

2 Did they finish their presentation?
　Yes ☐　　No ☐

If you don't send off your application today, you won't get the summer job.

3 Can Tom still get the summer job?
　Yes ☐　　No ☐

If you'd waited another day, you wouldn't have got the job.

4 Did Tom get the summer job?
　Yes ☐　　No ☐

b) Look at the pictures and tick the right answer. ___/ 2

Why didn't you bring your mobile?

1 If you'd brought your mobile, …
　A we could ring for help now. ☐
　B we couldn't ring for help. ☐

I hate this noise!

2 If they'd turned down the music, …
　A I would have called the police. ☐
　B I wouldn't have called the police. ☐

You should have locked the car.

3 If Amy had locked the car, …
　A the CD player wouldn't have been stolen. ☐
　B the CD player would have been stolen. ☐

Thanks again for helping me with Maths.

4 If Dave hadn't helped Julie,
　A she wouldn't have passed the Maths exam. ☐
　B she would have passed the Maths exam. ☐

16 GRAMMAR I would have stayed at home   /5

What would you have done differently?
Make short dialogues like the one in the picture.

> I went to school today, although I had a bad headache.

> I would have stayed at home.

1 **A:** Aidan walked back in the rain yesterday.

   B: (take the bus) _____

2 **A:** A boy fell off his bike in front of our house, but I didn't do anything.

   B: (phone for an ambulance) _____

3 **A:** John wanted to borrow my bike, but I said no.

   B: (lend it to him) _____

4 **A:** I couldn't do my Maths homework, so I went to school without it.

   B: (ask my mother) _____ to help me.

5 **A:** I stayed at the party although I was really tired.

   B: (leave and go to bed) _____

Lösungen

Unit 1 Australia

p. 7/8

1 Are Australian teenagers different?
a) **Charlene:**
15
reading / listening to music / tennis / swimming
travelling to Europe / studying (Biology) at the university
parents / friends (at tennis club) / (at school)
Dancing Queen by Abba / A song by Abba

Oscar:
15 / will be 16 next month
Melbourne
truck driver / drives a road train
waitress
surfing the net / (computer/chatting)
driving a road train
classmates / truck drivers
nothing special / anything except Abba

b) c
c) Individuelle Lösung

p. 8/9

2 Marine life
a) 1 fishing village
2 bits of fish the fishermen threw in the water / didn't have to go far for breakfast / could eat leftovers
3 in the 1980s
4 six to eight
5 females and babies / mums and kids
6 at the Visitor Centre
7 feed a dolphin a fish
8 to touch the dolphins

b) September 15th, December
9 am
Tuesdays, Thursdays, Saturdays, Sundays
$220
quite high / (usually) good

c) 1 a   2 c   3 c

p. 10

3 Why not go to Australia?
Individuelle Lösung

p. 10

4 International students in Australia
Individuelle Lösung

p. 11

5 Nice to meet you
Individuelle Lösung

p. 12/13

6 The "stolen generations"
a) Mögliche Lösung:
1 … her father took her to hospital because she was ill. From there she was taken to a home run by the church and never saw her parents again. (From then on people told her she was an orphan.)
2 … she lived in this home and was treated very badly by the people who ran it.
3 … she went to live with a family in Darwin who was nice to her.
4 … she got a letter from an aunt and learned that she wasn't an orphan and that her parents were alive and had been looking for her since she was five.

b) Mögliche Lösung:
1 … lonely and unhappy. The people who worked in the home sometimes beat her and didn't allow her too eat. They told her she was not as good as white people.
2 … lonely because she wasn't white like her new "parents" and the children at school weren't nice to her.
3 … terrible because everything that people had told her since she was five was a lie.

c) Individuelle Lösung

7 Sydney Explorer
True: 1, 2, 7
False: 4, 8
Not given: 3, 5, 6

p. 14/15

8 Sydney Harbour Highlights Cruise
1 90 minutes / 1.5 hours
2 Four
3 Sydney Harbour's Main Harbour / Sydney Opera House / Double Bay / Point Piper / Bradley Head / Sydney Harbour Bridge / Balmain / Darling Harbour
4 First-time visitors, families / (all travellers)
5 Circular Quay / Downtown Sydney
6 Circular Quay / Downtown Sydney / (where it starts / at the departure point)

p. 16/17

9 The Bridge Climb
1 October 1998
2 thunderstorms, strong winds
3 fantastic views of the harbour and city, up to the Pacific Ocean and the Blue Mountains
4 every day except 30 and 31 December
5 in advance for a specific time and date, online or on the telephone
6 three and a half hours
7 accompanied by an adult if between 10 and 15, older than 10, taller than 1.20 m
8 special suit over your clothes, rubber-soled shoes

p. 18/19

10 Extreme sports
Individuelle Lösung

p. 19

11 An e-mail from the outback
p. 20

Individuelle Lösung

12 Learning through travel
p. 20

Individuelle Lösung

13 At the lost property office
p. 21

Mögliche Lösung:
You	My friend has lost his digital camera.
You	Wann hast du sie das letzte Mal benutzt?
You	On the beach this morning.
You	Was für ein Modell ist sie und welche Farbe hat sie?
You	It's a Fuji in silver and pink.
You	So eine Kamera ist hier nicht.
You	Hast du bei der Station der Lebensretter gefragt?
You	No, he hasn't.
You	Wenn du die Kamera nicht findest, sollst du heute Abend wieder hier herkommen.
You	What time do you close?
You	Sie machen um 19 Uhr zu.
You	Thank you for your help. My friend / He hopes he can find his camera.

14 Signs
p. 22

a) Mögliche Lösung:

1 Auf dem ersten Schild steht, dass hier in der Gegend sehr giftige Pilze wachsen können, die man nicht essen darf. Wenn man denkt, dass man vielleicht doch so einen Pilz gegessen hat, soll man ins nächstgelegene Krankenhaus gehen.

2 Auf dem zweiten Schild steht, dass man all sein Obst hier in die Tonne werfen soll, bevor man in die fruchtfliegenfreie Zone weiterfährt. Fruchtfliegen können die Gemeinden Millionen von Dollar kosten.

3 Auf dem dritten Schild steht, dass der Weg gesperrt ist, weil es auf der Bergspitze stürmt.

4 Das Schild mit den Fahnen zeigt uns, wo wir schwimmen sollen: Zwischen den rot-gelben Fahnen. Dort passen Lebensretter auf. Wenn dunkle Fahnen wehen, ist es zu gefährlich, ins Wasser zu gehen. (Kinder müssen immer beaufsichtigt werden.)

b) Mögliche Lösung:

1 Dogs are not allowed on the playground. The playground is only allowed for children up to 15 years of age. You must put your rubbish in the bins. You have to be quiet here between 8 pm and 7 am.

2 When you are stopping here, turn off your engine.

3 Don't touch the objects.

4 Don't feed the animals.

15 Australia – the continent "Down Under"
p. 23

area divided into flag historical Aborigines diseases prisoners independent nationality/nationalities because of nearly outdoors cancer avoid

16 Preparing for a trip in Australia
p. 24

1 b 2 a 3 b 4 d 5 b 6 c

17 What did Rob do last week?
p. 25

a)

On Monday Rob usually plays cricket with his school team, but last Monday he went on a class trip.
On Tuesday Rob usually goes surfing, but last Tuesday he climbed a mountain.
On Wednesday Rob usually has surfing lessons, but last Wednesday he went fishing and canoeing.
On Thursday Rob usually watches a film at the cinema, but last Thursday he had a barbecue.
On Friday Rob usually goes swimming, but last Friday he went hiking.
On Saturday Rob usually plays tennis with his girlfriend Amy, but last Saturday he played tennis with a boy/classmate.
On Sunday Rob usually meets his friends at the beach, but last Sunday he met a group of tourists.

b) Individuelle Lösung

18 A phone call to Hong Kong
p. 26

Mögliche Lösung:

… she liked her life in the outback although sometimes she was a bit lonely.
She told me that she usually didn't get up before eight.
She went on to say she usually worked for school in the mornings.
She told me that last Monday she had ridden her motorbike to the dog fence to help her dad.
She went on to say that she had had to do her work for school in the evening.
She said that in June they were going on an excursion to a camp near Darwin.
She said she was really looking forward to seeing her classmates there.
She was sure they would have lots of fun.
She hoped the weather would be fine.

Unit 2 The world of work

p. 29/30 **1 Megan's work experience**
a) 1 Megan Smith
2 Mrs Carter
3 tomorrow / the following day at 11 am
4 turn left out of the exit, follow the road, hospital is right in front of her
b) 1 H 2 D 3 B 4 F 5 A
C, E und G passen nicht.
c) Megan Smith
Primary school
Secondary school
babysitting, newspaper round
volleyball, swimming
8 am to 7 pm
none
d) 1 b 2 a 3 c 4 b 5 d

p. 31/32 **2 Placements for work experience**
a) Jamie: *True:* 2, 3, 4, 5, 6 *False:* 1
Megan: *True:* 1, 2, 3, 5, 6 *False:* 4
b) 1 b 2 b 3 a 4 c 5 a 6 d

p. 33 **3 An interview**
Individuelle Lösung

p. 33 **4 A summer job**
Individuelle Lösung

p. 34/35 **5 A year as a volunteer in Doncaster**
True: 2, 4, 7, 11, 12
False: 3, 5, 10
Not given: 1, 6, 8, 9

p. 36 **6 Work experience – how it can help you**
1 C 2 A 3 E 4 B
D wird nicht verwendet.

p. 37 **7 Julia Meyer's report**
1 b 2 c 3 a 4 a

p. 38 **8 Work experience in Germany**
True: 2, 5, 7, 8
False: 1
Not given: 3, 4, 6

p. 38 **9 The right job for me**
Individuelle Lösung

p. 39 **10 A letter of application for a summer job**
Individuelle Lösung

11 A summer job in the USA p. 39
Mögliche Lösung:
Ich möchte gerne in den Sommerferien in Florida als Tennislehrer/in arbeiten. Ich könnte ab Juli dort in einem Sommercamp für Kinder arbeiten. Ich müsste vier bis sechs Trainingseinheiten am Tag leiten. Außerdem müsste ich einen Trainingsplan erstellen, den Tennisplatz fertigmachen und die Kinder während des Trainings beaufsichtigen. Die Arbeitszeit beginnt morgens um 9 Uhr und endet am Nachmittag. Ich hätte dann noch viel Zeit für Besichtigungen. Ich könnte vier bis sechs Wochen arbeiten und würde ungefähr $ 500 im Monat verdienen. Die Flugkosten werden auch bezahlt.

12 A summer job at a theme park p. 40
Mögliche Lösung:
You Er hat (in den Sommerferien) im Thorpe Park gearbeitet. Der Job hat ihm viel Spaß gemacht.
You How long did you have to work?
You Er musste von 10 Uhr morgens bis 6 Uhr abends arbeiten. Er musste auch am Wochenende arbeiten, weil da viel los war im Park.
You Did you have to do the same (kind of) work all the time?
You Nein, zuerst hat er bei der neuen Achterbahn gearbeitet, die richtig gruselig ist. Danach hat er Burger in einem der Restaurants verkauft.
You How much did you earn?
You £ 300 in vier Wochen.
You That's quite a lot. What did you like best?
You Die Freifahrten haben ihm am besten gefallen. Wenn die Karussells nicht zu voll waren, durften die Angestellten so oft fahren, wie sie wollten. Was ihm nicht gefallen hat, war mit Leuten sprechen zu müssen, die sich über die langen Schlangen vor den Fahrgeschäften beschwert haben.

13 Say it in English p. 41
Mögliche Lösung:
1 I don't mind working at the weekend.
2 I have filled in the form.
3 I'm happy to help my sister.
4 I used to be very excited/nervous when I had to take a test.
5 I'll let you know when I don't want the job.

p. 41 **14 What do they do?**
Mögliche Lösung:
1 Somebody who helps a vet.
2 Somebody who helps building houses.
3 Somebody who works in an office.
4 Somebody who works in a hospital.
5 Somebody who works at a garage and repairs cars.
6 Somebody who makes sure that people don't break the law.

p. 42 **15 Looking for a job**
1 c (advertisements)
2 application
3 surname/family name; birth
4 secondary
5 reference; contact
6 a (enclose)
7 suitably
8 weaknesses

p. 43 **16 An interview for a summer job**
went   were   was   needed   knew   had
worked / had worked   cleaned / had cleaned   wanted

p. 43 **17 The reality TV show**
1 … to wear suitable clothes.
2 … told them not to wear trendy clothes or jeans.
3 He told them not to sit down before they were offered a seat.
4 He told them not to talk too much.
5 He told them to prepare their answers before the interview.
6 He told them not to be afraid to ask questions of their own.
7 He told them to speak clearly and confidently.
8 He asked them to thank the interviewer before leaving.

18 At the tea shop   p. 44
a) 1 She asked me which school I went to.
2 She wanted to know what my favourite subjects were.
3 She asked me how many languages I could / was able to speak.
4 She asked me what my hobbies were.
5 She asked me what kind of work experience I had.
6 She asked me why I wanted to work in a tea shop.
b) 1 I asked her if/whether I would get some training before I started.
2 I asked her if/whether I could wear my own clothes to work.
3 I asked her if/whether she opened at the weekend.
4 I asked her if/whether I had to work on Sundays.
5 I asked her if/whether the tea shop was busy on Sunday afternoons.
6 I asked her if/whether I was allowed to eat some cake.

Unit 3   Teen world

p. 47/48 **1 Mark's friends**
a) 1, 3, 5, 6, 7, 9, 12
b) 1 a   2 b   3 c
c) Individuelle Lösung

p. 49/50 **2 Talking it over**
a) **Natalie:** travel agency
computer programmes
boys
parties, sleeping
Julie: Kid's Kitchen (Centre)
buy groceries/food, cook healthy meals
kids are interesting/fun
Saturday, 5 pm
in front of the church
shopping, cinema
b) **Jack:** go to the cinema, go to the park / go for a walk, have a coffee/pizza
Melanie: doesn't want a boyfriend / wants to have more time for her friends / wants to concentrate on her school work
c) 1 Saturday
2 ten
3 pizza, ice cream
4 (trendy) mobile phone
5 pink; MP3 player, camera
6 it's too expensive / Laura doesn't need it / it's just a toy / camera phones aren't good

3 Teenagers and their free time   p. 51
Individuelle Lösung

4 Voluntary work   p. 51
Individuelle Lösung

5 Boot Camps   p. 52/53
a) *Lines 1–4:* C
Lines 6–9: A
Lines 10–15: B
Lines 16–20: D
Lines 21–24: F
E wird nicht thematisiert.
b) individuelle Lösung

84 Lösungen

p. 54/55 **6 'TXT don't talk' say young people**
Mögliche Lösung:
a) 1 Not typical because over 80% of the young people use texting at least once a day.
2 Neither because just over 50% use texting more than 5 times a day.
3 Typical because less than 30% of young people end relationships by texting.
4 Not typical because only about 40% of young people make dates by texting.
b) 1 Not typical because over 60% of young people use their mobile phones, even when they are with friends.
2 Typical because under 20% of the young people in the survey talk quietly when they are using their mobile phones in public.
3 Typical because under 20% of young people leave their ring-tone on when they are in a cinema.
4 Not typical because nearly 80% of the young people said they could not live without their mobiles.

p. 56 **7 A letter to your headmaster**
Individuelle Lösung

p. 56 **8 A written discussion**
Individuelle Lösung

p. 57 **9 Applying for the Worldwide Voluntary Service**
Individuelle Lösung

p. 58 **10 How to use a cash machine**
Mögliche Lösung:
1 Jetzt die PIN eingeben und auf „enter" drücken.
2 Jetzt müsst ihr auf „British Pounds" drücken.
3 Heute kostet das Pfund € 1,15.
4 Wenn ihr eine Quittung wollt, müsst ihr „cash with receipt" drücken.
5 Jetzt müsst ihr den Betrag eingeben.
6 Jetzt müsst ihr auf „notes only" drücken, wenn ihr nur Scheine wollt, oder auf „notes and coins", wenn ihr Scheine und Münzen wollt.
7 Zieht jetzt die Karte raus.
8 Jetzt müsst ihr warten, bis das Geld kommt.
9 Jetzt zieht das Geld raus.
10 Jetzt zieht die Quittung raus.

11 In a mobile phone shop p. 59
Mögliche Lösung:
You It's € 99.90.
You Ist das Telefon gesperrt? / Hat das Handy einen SIM-Lock?
You No, it isn't blocked. You can use your old SIM-card or a new one.
You Mein Freund möchte das Handy kaufen. Kann er mit Kreditkarte bezahlen?
You Of course, you can.
You You have to keep the receipt.
You Kann er das Handy gleich benutzen? Er hat seine SIM-Card hier.
You Yes, but you have to enter your PIN first.

12 Paraphrasing p. 60
a) 1 alarm clock
2 busy
3 receipt
4 secretly
b) Mögliche Lösung:
1 A person who has no brothers or sisters
2 When you talk to someone in person/directly
3 To forbid sth.
4 Notes or coins

13 Odd word out p. 60
1 (to) punish: It is not a crime.
2 can: You cannot pay with it.
3 trash: The others are all sources of water.
4 court: It has not got anything to do with money.
5 behaviour: It is not a special day.

14 A presentation p. 61
has been collected   has been done   has been finished
have been built   has been repaired   have been bought
must be bought   must be installed   will be planted
must be found

Lösungen 85

Unit 4   Exploring cities

1   Movie talk
Boy's film
2 young man/boy/guy
3 American
4 India
5 BBC 2
The plot: 6, 7, 9, 11
14 Don't know

Girl's film
1 night before
2 poor/young guy
3 Indian
4 India
5 Movie Channel
The plot: 6, 7, 8, 10, 12
13 shocking / sad / sometimes funny
14 Yes

2   Getting to places
a) 1 in Hong Kong
   2 8 am to 11 pm
   3 by train
   4 the harbour, the mainland
   5 by bus, by tram
   6 walk around the city / go to a mall / have a cup of tea / walk to the harbour / watch the people and the ferries at the harbour
   7 very helpful
b) 1 tomorrow / the following day
   2 at Berlin Tegel / at Tegel Airport
   3 by taxi
   4 (about) 20 minutes
   5 (around) 20 euros
   6 he can walk
   7 by underground, by taxi
c) 1 b   2 c   3 d   4 c   5 c

3   Talking about photos
Individuelle Lösung

4   At the doctor's
Individuelle Lösung

5   A weekend in Berlin
Richtiger Plan: C
Zu unterstreichen:
In A: **Sunday pm** – shopping in Prenzlauer Berg, break in a café
In B: **Sunday pm** – visit the Jewish Museum and the Reichstag
In D: **Saturday pm** – walking tour of Berlin
In E: **Sunday pm** – walking tour of Berlin

6   Nelson Mandela
1 a   2 b   3 b   4 a   5 c   6 c   7 b   8 a
9 b   10 c

7   Life in big cities
Individuelle Lösung

8   My impressions of Mumbai and Johannesburg
Individuelle Lösung

9   Berlin – a great place to stay
Individuelle Lösung

10   Histmarol Cream
Mögliche Lösung:
1 bei Hautrötung, besonders nach Insektenstichen
2 nur äußerlich, nicht öfter als zweimal am Tag, nicht länger als fünf Tage
3 auf kaputter Haut, bei Allergie (gegen Antihistamine)
4 zwischen 4 °C und 25 °C, außerhalb der Reichweite von Kindern
5 Nicht in die Augen, Nase oder Mund gelangen lassen. Nicht bei Kindern unter 6 anwenden. Wenn die Schmerzen anhalten oder man Fieber bekommt, sofort einen Arzt aufsuchen.

11   At a youth hostel in Berlin
Mögliche Lösung:
You   Die beiden suchen ein Zweibett-Zimmer/ Doppelzimmer für eine Woche.
You   That's a bit difficult. You can have a double room tomorrow. For tonight he can only offer you two beds in the dormitory.
You   Die nehmen sie. Was kostet das? Ist das Frühstück inbegriffen?
You   A bed in the dormitory is €10 per night per person. The double room is €15. Breakfast is included. It's between 7 and 10 am.
You   Wo können sie duschen?
You   Toilets and showers are in the basement.
You   Can you both fill in the form and sign (it) at the bottom, please.
You   Here's the key for the dormitory at the end of the hall.

12   Words in combination I
a) (to) discover a polluted lake
   (to) eat at a fashionable restaurant
   (to) get financial help
   (to) know a glamorous movie star
   (to) speak an official language
   (to) wear colourful clothes
b) Individuelle Lösung

Lösungen

p. 76 **13 Words in combination II**
a) (to) adjust to
(to) be familiar with
(to) connect to/with
(to) draw sb.'s attention to
(to) give a talk on
(to) hold on
(to) lean out
(to) live on
on top of
typical of
b) 1 live on
2 on top of
3 lean out
4 adjust to
5 familiar with

p. 77 **14 Find the right words**
1 unemployment
2 suburb
3 freedom
4 survival
5 dormitory
6 confidence
7 shack
8 (to) separate
9 unforgettable
10 poverty
11 message

15 What if …? p. 78
a) 1 Yes 2 No 3 Yes 4 Yes
b) 1 A 2 B 3 A 4 A

16 I would have stayed at home p. 79
1 I would have taken the bus.
2 I would have phoned for an ambulance.
3 I would have lent it to him.
4 I would have asked my mother (to help me).
5 I would have left and gone to bed.

Quellenverzeichnis

Illustrationen
Carlos Borrell, Berlin (S. 10 oben); **Katharina Wieker**, Berlin (S. 7; 8; 11; 22 oben Bild 1–4; 25; 26; 42; 44; 58; 78; 79)

Bildquellen
Alamy, Abingdon (S. 20 re.: Paul Kingsley; S. 61: peter dench); **Corbis**, Düsseldorf (S. 10 2. v. oben li.: L. Clarke; S. 18 unten: Atlantide Phototravel); **Images.de**, Berlin (S. 22 unten Bild 2: Eberhard Grames); **iStockphoto**, Calgary (S. 10 unten li.: josef volavka, 2. v. unten re.: William Ross-Jones; S. 19 Mitte: mayo5, re.: Krzysztof Chrystowski; S. 41 Mitte: Justin Horrocks, re.: Gary Douglas-Beet; S. 69 2. v. oben: 4x6); **Picture Alliance**, Frankfurt/Main (S. 10 2. v. unten li.: Dallas and John Heaton/Spectrum; S. 18 oben: Bildagentur-online/BL-McPhoto; S. 22 unten Bild 3: ZB; S. 67 unten: dpa; S. 71: dpa); **Schapowalow**, Hamburg (S. 67 oben: Robert Harding); **Shutterstock**, New York (S. 10 oben li.: Paul Burdett, oben re.: Lee Torrens, 2. v. oben re.: clearviewstock, unten re.: Neale Cousland; S. 14 li.: IRP, re.: Leah-Anne Thompson; S. 19 li.: 2happy; S. 20 li.: Pete Niesen, Mitte: Arek Rainczuk; S. 39: James Peragine; S. 41 li.: Monika Wisniewska, 2. v. li.: Dean Mitchell, 2. v. re.: Stephen Coburn; S. 49 li.: Monkey Business Images, re.: MikLav; S. 69 oben: Valua Vitaly, Mitte: cenker atila, 2. v. unten: Suzanne Tucker, unten: A Turner); **ullstein bild**, Berlin (S. 22 unten Bild 4: Imagebroker.net); **Vario Images**, Bonn (S. 22 unten Bild 1); **Viator.com**, San Francisco (S. 16)

Titelbild
Corel Library (Hintergrund Australian Flag)

Textquellen
S. 14 Sydney *Explorer Hop-on-Hop-off sightseeing bus*. Abridged and adapted from: "Sydney Explorer Hop-on-Hop-off sightseeing bus". From http://www.sydney buses.info/tourist-services/sydney-explorer.htm. (Stand: 04.02.10); **S. 16** *Sydney Harbour Highlights Cruise*. Abridged from: "Sydney Harbour Highlights Cruise". From http://www.viator.com/tours/Sydney/Sydney-Harbour-Highlights-Cruise/d357-3378HIGH, Used with permission of viator.com, San Francisco. (Stand: 04.02.10); **S. 36** *Work experience – how it can help you*. From: http://www.direct.gov.uk/en/Education AndLearning/14To19/Years10And11/DG_10013569, © Crown copyright. (Stand: 04.02.10); **S. 38** *Work experience in Germany. Text A*. Abridged and adapted from "Higginson and Kirby work experience". From http://www.ukgermanconnection.org/cms/?location_id= 1311. (Stand: 26.02.10), *Work experience in Germany. Text B*. Abridged and adapted from "Scholarships Photo Diary. Taken during the scholarships programme 2008". From http://www.ukgermanconnection.org/cms/?location_id=570. (Stand: 26.02.10); **S. 52** *Boot Camps*. Abridged from "Boot Camp" by Todd Strasser, used with permission of the author.